NEW WORK O

CHRISTINE INGHAM

New Work Options
How to keep your career buoyant
in turbulent times

Thorsons
An Imprint of HarperCollins*Publishers*

Thorsons
An Imprint of HarperCollins*Publishers*
77–85 Fulham Palace Road,
Hammersmith, London W6 8JB
1160 Battery Street,
San Francisco, California 94111-1213

Published by Thorsons 1996
10 9 8 7 6 5 4 3 2 1

A catalogue record for this book
is available from the British Library

ISBN 0 7225 3183 4

Printed in Great Britain by
HarperCollinsManufacturing Glasgow

Contents

Introduction

Great changes have been taking place over recent years on the workplace front. The security we had previously taken for granted – a regular job being there for us when we needed one – has all but disappeared. Although this is an unsettling picture, the changes which have been taking place are also throwing up new ways of working, new work options. But how do we take advantage of them?

With any new situation in which we find ourselves, in any aspect of life, we always go through a learning curve. This is where most of us are right now, whether trying to enter, re-enter or remain in the job market. The new face of work has changed, that much we know, but how are we to cope with it? This is the aim of *New Work Options*. It is about trying to help us understand and make sense of what we see going on around us. It is about looking at the new options which are emerging, and creating new opportunities for ourselves. It is about what you can do to make these new options work *for* you, not against you.

To get a better feel of what each option might really be like, I have spoken to many people who are already working in the 'new' ways. They talk about their own experiences and the advantages and disadvantages they have come across. They offer sound words of advice to others who might be interested in working in the same way they do. Nothing can speak so well as the voice of experience.

For myself, I too have experience of a number of the work

options mentioned: working abroad, the voluntary sector, self-employment, contract work – all culminating in a portfolio career. I now would not have it any other way.

Hopefully *New Work Options* will help you identify options which open new doors for you, and enable you to see how you can begin to make the new options work to your advantage.

Happy reading; and happy new working.

CHAPTER ONE

All Change

In the beginning was the Word. And the Word was *flexibility*. So began the workplace revolution. And so, for many of us, began the confusion.

It now seems that the security which came from having a regular job has, almost overnight, been taken away from us. None of us can any longer take our employment status for granted. What was once a firm intention to stay put in a job, or with an organization, until *we* chose to move on has been swept aside and into the garbage can, an impossible dream for most of us.

It is not as though we are not used to change. New technology develops rapidly and finds its way into our lives on a regular basis, but it seems amazing to the majority of us who are of working age that such great changes have taken place, seemingly so quickly, in employment. Past practices are gone; the present seems confusing, the future frightening.

Management and businesses may know where they are going and understand why any changes have been taking place, but information is slow to filter down to the people who feel the effects most keenly. We, the working population, are less aware of the whys and wherefores. All we know is that things have changed, and most of us do not know how to cope or adapt. All we know for sure is what the media has been telling us in the now well-worn phrase, 'The nine-to-five job for life is a thing of the past.' No wonder we feel confused.

This ball of confusion needs to be unravelled. Like a tangle of wool, it is impossible to see its potential until you find the beginning and end, smooth out the knots in between then lay it out to enable you to see what can be made of it. In the same way, a box full of rough bits and pieces of wood, metal, screws, nails and brackets may make you shriek 'What a load of junk,' until you have rummaged through, sorted it all out into piles, and can see what could be made out of the confusion which previously had been before you.

Similarly, it may help to dispel these chaotic feelings if we have a proper look at how the recent changes have come about.

How We Got Here

Throughout the middle years of the twentieth century those who could go out to work, did. A full 90 per cent of the workforce was employed in jobs which were of the nine-to-five variety, where the work performed was carried out in the normal place of work. These were the days when, in the main, termination of employment happened only when it was time to move on, either into another job or on to retirement.

The unending regularity of the established work pattern may be something which the next generation will come only to wonder at. But with the changes which businesses have undergone, the figure of 90 per cent has altered dramatically. For example, in the early 1990s research was suggesting that in the UK a staggering 75 per cent of the workforce had some form of flexibility in their work pattern. A regular, full-time job now appears to be available only for the minority; the rest of the 'regular' job opportunities have been swept aside somewhere along the way.

The tide of change which has crashed over the firm foundation of regular employment appears to have come in many waves:

Recession

Now more than ever, competition in the business world is global – and fierce. Only the strong, resilient and shrewd survive these days. With an eye on the preservation of profit margins, businesses have had to look long and hard at areas where savings could be made, while they battle on the other flank with sometimes volatile interest rates, fluctuating exchange rates, and hostile competitors as far afield as the other side of the world.

Eagle eyes were cast across all areas of expenditure. Nothing escaped inspection, until finally the people who made up the business itself came under scrutiny. They had to. Labour costs constitute major overheads in any business; they therefore also offer the potential for major savings.

The squeeze was on.

In a recent white paper on European social policy, the European Commission suggests that 'Flexibility in working time should be acknowledged, particularly at company level as part of developing new patterns of work and in order to improve competitiveness and increase employment opportunities.' Governments, in an attempt to reinforce the message, have begun to cry out at every opportunity that in order to be competitive, flexibility must be the order of the day. In the UK in 1993, the Chancellor of the Exchequer also said that he saw improved flexibility as being the answer to the ongoing problem of unemployment. Flexibility appeared to be the new cure-all.

Two new terms crept into the business world: *numerical flexibility* and *functional flexibility*. The first refers to the ability of employers to expand and contract their workforce quickly, in response to work demands. Functional flexibility refers to multi-skilling employees so that they are able to switch easily from one task, or function, to another instead of being limited to just one area of expertise.

The word flexibility began to enter into people's consciousness, although initially I would guess that we, the majority, thought it probably did not apply to us. After all, we were in a secure, regular, full-time job, weren't we?

New Technology

The continuing introduction of new technology has facilitated many changes in the workplace. Sometimes this has meant jobs being replaced in their entirety by machines where, for example, robots have come into their own to replace the robotic action of assembly line workers. It has also meant that some workers need no longer work in the same place as everyone else. Working away from the office has opened up many new job opportunities in the field of teleworking.

Trades Unions

In the UK, legislation in the 1980s quashed the strong power which the unions had held up until then. Formerly, at the merest hint of removing closed shop practices there would emerge the threat of strike action. The unions were able to hold management captive in an attempt to maintain job security for their members. But the changes in legislation loosened the grip of the unions, and businesses became free to adopt more flexible work practices.

The unions have been instrumental in pushing through reductions in the number of hours worked per week. Although this obviously came as a welcome change for employees, businesses were left with the problem of how to make up the short-fall in production. If the factory staff were working two hours less each week, how could the orders possibly be filled on time? How would production targets be met?

Faced with this dilemma, businesses were forced to look at alternative ways of maintaining production while offsetting any potential increases in costs for additional labour.

Demographic Changes

As the baby-boom generation reaches middle age, what is left in its wake is a drop in the number of school-leavers entering the job

4

market. Concerned at the level of unemployment they see around them, many are choosing to stay on at school past the official school-leaving age. Increasing numbers are also continuing on into further and higher education, shrinking the number of new entrants to the job market even more.

As this shortage feeds through, employers are realizing that they need to look elsewhere to recruit. The growing number of women entering the workforce and the burgeoning numbers of active but retired people offer possibilities. However, the needs of people in either of these two categories can be very different. Having work which fits in with other commitments or lifestyle requirements has meant that alternative work practices have had to develop in order to attract and retain such individuals. Being in employment, for some, has to fit in with childcare, caring responsibilities or leisure pursuits. Employers have therefore had to respond and change.

The 24-hour Global Society

Migrations towards a 'We never close' society, at which the Americans are already perceived as being past masters, means new staffing challenges and work opportunities. People want to shop when it suits them, be it after shift-working when most other people are still asleep, in the evening after working parents have had their 'quality' time with their families, or throughout the weekend, at times previously held sacrosanct. The demand for longer opening times means that employees are now needed outside 'regular' working hours.

The same situation arises in some industries where rapid response to customers in other time zones is necessary. Businesses are bargain hunting worldwide to find the best price for the job – even if that means an American company using workers in India to produce documentation for them.

In the smaller societies of yesteryear, employers had only to concern themselves with opening the business doors at nine o'clock in the morning and then closing them again at end of day.

Now, in order to respond to the changing world around them a flexible approach to staffing is a necessity. In turn, this becomes a self-perpetuating phenomenon. As more businesses operate outside 'normal' hours, more staff are needed to work during those periods, who then also require access to services at times which are out of step with the previous nine-to-five provision. And so it goes on.

Implications for Business

Businesses have had it tough. Many have been taken to the edge of the precipice, peered over and seen the unsightly remains of those who have not managed to halt the slide on to the rocks of bankruptcy and closure. Fearing lest that happen to them too, businesses have had to resort to action – radical action. The way they have organized themselves for decades has been scrutinized and seen for what it was: a financial albatross preventing them from being able to do the things which are now being demanded of them if they are to survive. They have to be able to cut overheads and keep them low, to find new ways to respond quickly to demand, to cope with fluctuations in work and demand which are so much a part of business life today, and to go 'back to basics' and reconnect with the core function of their business, whether this is building computers or selling dishwashers.

The result has been a radical redesign of staffing structures. New technology has enabled many changes to be introduced which have reduced the number of people needed in some areas of work. With companies turning their focus back on to their core activities they have identified where savings could be made, such as by closing whole departments concerned with cleaning, maintenance and catering, and off-loading the work on to contractors' shoulders.

The workforce has shrunk even further as all but the most essential staff members have been eliminated. Previously, where the number of people employed full-time reflected an anticipation of peak-time demands, now only a skeleton crew is kept on; the peak periods being covered by staff who are brought in as required. Businesses are becoming far more reluctant to meet the cost of retaining staff when there is not necessarily enough work to keep them occupied for the full working week.

The fluctuations with which business has to cope cover a wide range:

- unpredictable demands – new orders, cancellations, new trends, changes in legislation, new projects
- daily demands – staff levels must be flexible to cover lunch-times, evening work, commuter time
- weekly demands – changing staff numbers for weekends, pay-days, school days, slack days, delivery days
- monthly demands – taking on staff for regular administrative chores such as those relating to accounts, salary payments, etc.
- yearly demands – having to bring in (or let go of) staff during tax periods, accounting periods, peak seasons, off-seasons, as a result of weather-related hold-ups, academic sessions, governmental sessions.

The fluctuations experienced by any one organization depend upon the nature of the business, its location, size and so on. But what many have come to understand is that keeping staff on a full-time and permanent basis may not always be the most profitable way to manage their activities.

To maximize the investment in plant and premises, many businesses have started to operate outside 'normal' working patterns – for example, cutting down on non-productive start-up and close-down times by keeping plants in use for a greater number of hours.

And so, overall what have developed are structures in businesses which are very different from the pyramid-style organizations we had all come to understand, with Big Boss sitting at the top and the many minions stretched out along the bottom but part of the organization all the same. What has developed is more akin to a flower than a pyramid. Within the centre, like the yellow eye of a daisy, is a solid core of permanent staff. It is much smaller than the business as a whole, but it represents the essential people: the professionals with the skills, knowledge and training necessary to keep the business activities in full flow. These people are mainly full-time, holding down jobs which belong to what we might describe as the 'old style' pattern of work. They have job security (or as much as one might expect these days), have access to training and to promotion and career prospects; they also enjoy company benefits.

Outside of this core are what are now called the *peripheral* workers; they are those who rest on the petals of the organizational flower; petals which can be dropped and detached from the core whenever the work supply drops to a level which makes keeping them on unnecessary – even undesirable. Inevitably the people in this category have no job security, no prospects, little access to training or any other benefits bestowed by the company on those in the core. Perhaps one day soon comments like these may be heard: 'Hey, I've joined the core,' and 'Well, Martin, I've decided at last to go peripheral.'

In this novel structure employers have found themselves with a new function. As Charles Handy points out in his book *The Empty Raincoat*, managers now have to fulfil the new role they have created for themselves: that of organizers. They have to organize and respond to the constantly changing peripheral staffing requirements, rather than simply oversee permanent staff – who now constitute just one much smaller section of the workforce.

As this phenomenon evolves we are left wondering whether this new breed of employers might ultimately lose sight of any responsibilities they may have to the people in the developing peripheral section of the workforce. Might it lead to exploitation? Might it lead to a view of people as mere work-fodder? But if so, might it also in the course of time backfire on those employers careless enough not to value the input from each and every one of their workers, be they core or peripheral? Equally, it may not take too long for people to come to the realization that, as peripheral workers, they are still in demand, still needed, even if not by the same business all the time. And perhaps it will not take long for peripheral workers to get to know which businesses have the best organizational structures for them. They will know which ones to choose to work for and which ones to leave well alone. Who will be the winners and losers then?

What Is Flexibility?

So far we have seen how businesses have felt the need to look at options which can increase their flexibility and therefore their competitiveness, whether this is because of the introduction of new technology, in order to attract applicants to fulfil its recruitment needs, or to respond to production, profitability or customer demands. Many businesses have now adopted, to a greater or lesser degree, the core/peripheral structure and applied it to their workforce. But are we simply talking about the introduction of part-time work or shift-work?

The permutations and combinations which have developed over recent years would have amazed our Victorian work-orientated predecessors, who were no slouches themselves when it came to inventiveness. Here are some of them:

- Zero-hours contracts: a contract with an employer with no guarantee of even a minimum number of hours of paid work
- Short-term contracts: where you are employed for a set duration in either a part-time or full-time capacity, but without the benefits of being a permanent member of staff
- Teleworking: working at home using telecommunications tools to enable you to carry out your work
- Part-time work
- Job sharing: where two people fill a post previously occupied by one person
- Nine-day fortnights
- Flexitime: where an agreed number of hours are worked, at any time over an agreed period
- Term-time working: enabling people with children to work only during term time

- V-time: where an agreed number of hours are voluntarily reduced over a period of time
- Sabbaticals: an extended period of leave, normally offered to long-service staff
- Career breaks: taken by employees with the understanding that they will be able to re-enter employment with the company at an agreed future date
- Temporary working (temping)
- Outsourcing: putting out to competitive tender non-core activities, such as sub-contracting the catering function to outside caterers.

Some of the flexible options now available benefit the workforce as well as the employer. Some options offer more job security than others. All of them have been introduced in situations where the business concerned will benefit in the long run, whether by retaining staff in whom they have invested training and whose skills they value (as with career breaks), or by introducing a tele-working scheme to cut down on the costs of office space and overheads. All are the result of the drive for continuing productivity and profitability. At the end of the day it may be incidental to the business if the workforce benefits or not.

The Personal Dimension

Although a number of the flexible options (such as term-time working) benefit some individuals, other people have found themselves confronted with work patterns with which they are unfamiliar and which they see as unwelcome. Gone is the safety and security of the normal work-a-day routine. Gone is the structure to their working lives upon which they may have come to depend. A new world of work has opened up before them – but what, they wonder, is lying in wait?

Freed from the shackles of the nine-to-five, we might imagine we would relish our newfound sense of freedom. That may have been true when the freedom was temporary and limited to the two weeks' summer holiday when we could really 'get away from it all'. However, like someone who has become unemployed, many of us find it unthinkable that there is now no longer a parental-like tie to bind us until retirement to a father/mother figure employer. We no longer have them telling us when to go to work for ever. They have cast us aside out of the warm security of parental arms. And that not only hurts; it is scary, too. It makes demands on us that we never thought we would have to experience – or cope with. The situation demands that our relationship with employers change, and in turn we too must change.

A lot is expected of those of us in the present working population. We are the ones having to break new ground and learn how best to handle this new situation. The real difficulty arises because we are a new generation of workers and have as yet few, if any, role models close to hand. Instead, we sit on the sidelines holding hands with other like-minded souls, wondering what on earth we are going to do.

It seems that the only practical thing we can do is what our employers have previously done for us: accept the responsibility. This new situation means we can no longer sit back comfortably in the work carriage as it takes us onward, perhaps upward, and into retirement. We now have to take the reins ourselves. This has never been demanded of us before, and it can seem a frightening prospect.

Developments in the job market, plus our own experience, are now telling us that our mindset must change from 'I want a full-time job like I used to have' or 'I want a secure job like he's/she's got'. We have to rethink our working time and lives, perhaps quite radically. Some of us may have little option but to start to find more acceptable and manageable solutions.

As we begin to consider what opportunities we can make for ourselves, we may discover that options become more far-ranging than we at first anticipated. Instead of considering how to redefine just our working lives, we may start to realize that this also enables us to reshape our non-working lives too, into something which has equal, if not more, benefits than we have ever before experienced when working in a regular pattern of employment.

The responsibilities inherent in taking on such a task are not to be underestimated, however. We, not our employers, may now have to cope with the problem of not having enough work to fill a working week or year. We are now the ones to feel the insecurity of not having a pay-packet coming in, regardless of how many customers walk through the door. We may be the ones to shoulder the overheads normally incumbent on employers. The benefits we previously took for granted we now have to address for ourselves. As Handy points out, 'Conditioned to life as employees, we now expect them [the workforce] to be entrepreneurs.' Being in the peripheral workforce and managing successfully can indeed demand a certain degree of entrepreneurial flair. What was previously our employers' 'business' is now ours. It is up to us to keep a positive cashflow (a wage packet coming in) and an eye out for new customers (where the next job is coming from). It may indeed demand of us skills which seem more akin to those of someone who is self-employed.

In order to survive, one thing is certain: we must be more pro-active. The spoon-feeding is over; we must go out into the wide world and forage for our food by ourselves. It means we will have to develop new skills, new life-skills; we must develop an eye for an opportunity and be willing to consider options we have never needed to consider before.

The desire for the security of a regular nine-to-five job for life may never disappear, but perhaps what many of us have learned in recent years is that the security was never really there in the first place. It was a sham, a charade, a mirage. Even banking and law, two professions previously held to be among the most secure, have fallen prey to the recession. People who thought they would never be out of a job are having to look again at the assumptions they held dear.

It seems that the only way to survive in these challenging times is to play the game to suit ourselves. Initially it may seem that no benefits could possibly be had in this new working world – but they are there. They may not be the same benefits as before, but that is not to say they are of inferior quality; indeed, some are of a higher calibre than we may have thought possible.

Defining your own path for the rest of your working life is an opportunity not to be missed. Where do you want to be in five, ten, twenty years' time? What would you like to experience along the way? How would you like your other commitments to fit in with your working life? How would you and your partner like to share between you the income-generating and non-income-generating work? What opportunities would you like to consider which might otherwise have been cast aside while you rested securely in your nine-to-five life?

It is strange for many of us to start rethinking our working and non-working lives so radically. It requires us to find new ways. In order to do so we need to learn the rules of this new game, to work out how it can be played – to suit our own personal situation – and even to make up some of the rules ourselves. Hopefully the rest of this book will enable you to do this. We will look at a wide range of opportunities, many of which may have been unavailable to you before. The door on the nine-to-five might be closing, but other, potentially more exciting doors are opening.

CHAPTER TWO

Portfolio Careers

As the workplace revolution has developed, new words are beginning to creep into our language: *portfolio* is one such word.

What is a portfolio career? Put simply, it is a collection of jobs held by one person. This approach to employment is radically different from what most of us have come to know. In the past our job of work has mainly restricted us to one employer – the old 'job for life' idea. But with recent developments people are beginning to realize that, although the idea may still be desirable, there are other alternatives emerging. Having a portfolio approach to work is one such alternative.

Why It Has Evolved

As we have already seen, full-time jobs have been disappearing as businesses desperately try to find new solutions to weather the problems of world-wide recession. Global competitiveness, changing demographics and new technology have all played their part. As a result, businesses have had to look at ways in which they can utilize their workforce while cutting overheads, maximizing productivity and retaining its skilled professionals. One of the ways in which they have done this is by shedding full-time posts – and creating part-time ones in their place.

The benefits for the companies are clear, although more

financially rewarding in some countries than others. Various national governments have created a range of financial incentives to employers in order to entice them into creating more part-time vacancies. For example, in France employers pay a reduced Social Security contribution for creating new part-time vacancies, or for converting full-time posts to part-time ones. In the UK, employers pay no Social Security contributions for employees who earn below a certain minimum, thus encouraging them to have more part-time employees on their books and to increase the number of those whose wages are below that minimum.

Reflecting these changes, part-time vacancies across Europe increased by approximately 25 per cent between 1987 and 1992, during which time the number of part-time employees increased by over 3.3 million; an average yearly increase of over 660,000 workers. Similarly, the US has also seen increases: between 1990 and 1994 they experienced an increase in part-time workers of over 17 per cent, resulting in over 23.25 million people engaged in part-time work – over 18 per cent of the total number of people in work. However, percentage-wise this is small fry compared with the Netherlands, which leads the table: in 1991 32 per cent of employees were in part-time work. In the UK approximately 25 per cent were part-time, while this figure stood at 23 per cent in Australia.

Interestingly, the division between men and women in part-time employment is almost without exception weighted towards women, presumably related to the fact that so many wish to combine paid employment with child-rearing – and that women tend to be paid less than men and are therefore cheaper to hire. However, in some countries the picture appears to be changing. In the US the number of men in part-time employment between 1990 and 1994 rose by over 25 per cent, while the number of women increased at a slower rate (approximately 15 per cent). Similarly, in the UK during 1993 the number of men in part-time employment increased by almost 10 per cent, while the number of women increased by only 3 per cent. This trend may also reflect a sea-change in people's attitudes to working at other than a traditional full-time job. It would appear that working part-time is becoming more socially acceptable.

In Denmark, a blue-collar union's own survey discovered that twice as many of its members who were already working part-time were interested in part-time work. This sort of change in attitude may be due to many factors, not least of which that while part-time vacancies have traditionally been in mainly unskilled work, there are now signs that more senior part-time positions are being created. In the UK, professionals across a wide range are moving into part-time posts, including doctors, police and top civil servants. And while each country reports that the *majority* of part-timers are in unskilled or semi-skilled work, that still leaves a number of people in the skilled/managerial/professional category.

Perhaps people are realizing that there is something between the two end-points of full-time work and unemployment. There may be advantages for employers in having more part-time staff, but perhaps employees are realizing the benefits to be had by them, too.

And so, with the undoubted growth in part-time work, the opportunities to create a portfolio of different jobs emerge. A suitable nine-to-five vacancy might be a long time coming these days, but in the meantime a full-time equivalent could be devised through amassing a collection, or portfolio, of different part-time jobs.

It has been frustrating for people who are unemployed when they come to scan the job advertisements only to find part-time vacancies advertised. 'That's not what I'm looking for!' many have cried in dismay. Indeed, a single part-time job is obviously no substitute for a full-time one. But the chink in the armour to this seemingly unconquerable dilemma is that, although one bit of part-time work might seem useless on its own, a combination of two or more may be the answer. Here are the experiences of two people who decided to go down this particular route:

The Portfolio Experience

Ali is 32 years old and single. He has worked previously as a co-project worker in a community café which employs and assists people with learning difficulties. Due to the threat of cuts to its funding, Ali decided to start looking for other jobs – a case of jumping before he was pushed.

I didn't start off planning to have two part-time jobs; I was looking for full-time work at first and started by contacting a High Street chain-store in the November because I knew there'd be Christmas work. I also thought that because I'd worked for them before on a full-time permanent basis, and my record with them was very good, that they would take me on full-time. But then I learned at the recruitment evening that they don't take on full-timers anymore. I was told there'd be extra hours for the part-timers to work, so I thought I'd better take what was available. I did do extra hours over Christmas but my basic hours were part-time: 17 hours 45 minutes.

After Christmas I started job-searching again for full-time work but nothing came up. Then I realized that because there were so many job shares and part-time vacancies, more so than full-time, I thought 'why not keep the job I've got and find something else to make up a full-time wage?' So I went for a number of jobs and then this one came up working with a voluntary organization for 15 hours a week, again with people with learning difficulties – and I got it. It fitted in well with the other one. I worked three hours a day at the voluntary place, starting at 10 o'clock and finishing at 1 o'clock. I'd get home for 2 o'clock and then I'd leave my house about 3 o'clock to get to the other job for 4.30 p.m., so time-wise it just fitted. It was a little bit tight some days when they wanted me in that bit earlier at the store, but I was never late.

Really I only worked at the store to keep me away from the dole queue; and because it was part-time and the hours with the voluntary organization were quite flexible I could work one with the other. But I knew that at the end of the day my real commitment was to the voluntary work. The other one was just supporting it and helping me get a better wage at the end of the week.

So I took the job at the voluntary place even though it was only 15 hours. If I'd turned it down I would have been refusing the opening I wanted, so I knew I had to do it to get a foot in the door. It was an opening and I thought, 'well, from there, who knows?' Essentially I took it because I knew I'd learn more and so it was good for me even though it was only going to be 15 hours a week. I knew I wanted to gain as much experience as possible, and thought that perhaps when I felt comfortable about what I'd learned, and gained enough knowledge, I'd go and look elsewhere for a full-time job in the social field.

Coping with two jobs instead of just the one is a new concept to most people, who are more used to the idea of having only the one place of work to go to. I asked Ali about any problems he had encountered in balancing the two jobs he had.

I did find it difficult having two different types of jobs; switching off from one and then mentally trying to click on to the next was hard because the two jobs were completely different. The only thing that was similar is that they both involved people, but they were very different: helping people with disabilities in one job and then being a sales assistant in the other.

There was also quite a bit of travelling involved. It doesn't sound a lot but when I put it into practice it was hard. I wasn't getting home until 8.30/8.45 p.m. most evenings, and even later on Thursdays when I worked late at the store. So although I was working the hours just short of a standard week, i.e. 32, the working day for me was a lot longer; it was a 12-hour day if you included the travel time. I also worked every Saturday at the store, so I only got one full day off a week. It was quite stressful knowing you only had one day off to do all the laundry, etc. and still try and rest and have time to yourself and have some sort of social life as well. The ordinary things you take for granted in the day did come under a certain amount of strain. I didn't realize at the time just how tired it was making me until I stopped doing it. Now when I look back I think 'how did I do that?' But then you do it when you know you have to.

It also cost me more money having the two jobs. Because I was rushing around so much I was buying convenience foods precisely because it was more convenient for me. I would buy lunch from a sandwich bar so that I didn't have to think about getting to a supermarket each week, buying in shopping and making sandwiches at night for the following morning. I was too tired to think about all that. I just thought, 'it's convenient for me to spend the money,' so it was quite expensive.

Although it did have its down side for Ali because of the travelling involved in getting from one job to the other, it did eventually pay off in the long term. As can often happen, Ali's part-time job at the voluntary organization eventually turned into full-time and it came about because he used his initiative. He decided to approach the organization's committee with figures showing how much extra time he had been putting in and what work there was for him to do, and then requested that they agree to increasing his hours – which they did.

Now they've given me more hours it was well worth taking the part-time job although I can't say I knew that at the time. I'm better off now, working full-time, and I was better off having the two part-time jobs than being on the dole. On reflection I might have had more money if I'd kept just the one part-time job because of how the Social Security benefits worked at the time, but I didn't want to fall into that rat-trap. I know I'm the sort of person who could get a bit lazy and end up thinking 'well, what's the point, everything's getting paid for. I'm not used to having pots of money, so why not let the State pay me and I'll just keep on with the one job?' But that's not really encouraging for myself. I wanted to make things better for myself. The State can't do that for me; they can only help. I thought, 'no I've got to go out and look. I don't want to rely on benefits to pay my rent. I want to pay my rent, and I want to work for the money.'

Ali has learned a lot from his experience of holding down two jobs at once, and I asked him what key points people should consider before they decide to go down this route.

One out of the two jobs must be flexible. It gives you a certain amount of leeway if, like me, you're relying on public transport to take you between jobs. You do tend to be clock-watching quite a lot, so having flexibility in one of the jobs helps you juggle things around and make life easier. For example, the hours at the voluntary place were reasonably flexible so I knew that if I was going to be late I could make it up some other time.

I think you have to analyse exactly the nature of the work you want to do. It's got to be something you're going to enjoy, because once you've come off benefits it's going to be hard to get back on.

It's also worth having a portfolio of jobs even if only one of them is going to take you to the goal you want.

I'd say try it. It eventually can pay dividends and, from a prospective employer's point of view, it looks good on your CV. It must show you're willing and keen, and if this is the way into another job and to increase your learning, then go for it.

Ultimately it paid dividends for Ali. Taking on one job just for the money meant he could use it as a spring-board to finding a second one, one which he had been holding out for. Although the job he really wanted was initially only 15 hours a week, it was a good move for him to take it since it eventually led him into a full-time position. It might never have happened if he had not actually been in the post, proving his worth and showing his managers that the project he was working on would benefit from an increase in his hours. His long-term strategy paid off.

For Helga the situation was rather different. She lives in a rural area and is married with two children. She wanted to return to work after her last child had started school. She says her 'mix and match' of jobs is ideal for her and she thoroughly enjoys them.

Initially I went for a job that I wasn't actually trained in – it was a part-time packing job for a mail order company. The manager phoned me up and said 'You're obviously too qualified just to be packing. We've got a job on the computers doing the invoicing. Do you want it?' So I said 'Yes.' That was the first [part-time] job that I got and it was a real advantage that it was actually in town.

Previous to getting that job I had sent a speculative letter to a home for elderly people where I live locally, and said that if they had a receptionist's job I'd be interested, but they didn't have one. I knew they had recently advertised for an entertainments officer but I thought it was at weekends which I didn't want. Anyway, the woman that got it was only there probably less than a year when the job came up again. They didn't really want to advertise because of all the hassle, so basically I got a phone call asking if I would be interested in the job. It turned out it didn't entail weekends and they wanted someone for just the afternoons. I only worked mornings at the other place, apart from a Wednesday when they wanted me on reception all day when their PA wasn't there, so I asked my first boss if he could find someone to cover for me on Wednesdays. As it turned out, the other woman who was on the computers wanted a bit of overtime, so the three hours I lost she took over, and it all sort of slotted into place. It's worked out quite well.

I do 9 a.m. to 12 noon in one job, come home, have lunch, and get changed (because I have a uniform with the second job) and then I go back from 1 p.m. until 4 p.m. I wouldn't have wanted to work any later than 4 o'clock because I've always said that I would be at home for the children.

I really wanted the job at the home because it was something so different and I wanted to have a go and see how I got on, how I enjoyed it. Had it been another office job I perhaps wouldn't have gone for it. And I think that, in a way, by having the two part-time jobs if at any time you have any problems with one you've always got the other one to fall back on.

Apart from being able to combine her work with being there for her children, Helga particularly enjoys the departure from the norm in having more than just one job.

It's nice having two jobs because you don't get bored. If you've got one job and it's nine-to-five I think you tend to get bored or fed up, whereas if you have two you've got the variety, and mine are so different as well. I mean, with one I'm sitting in front of the computer, and with the other I'm arranging entertainments for the residents of the home. One is with paper and the other with people, so I think in a way I've got the best of both worlds.

Portfolio working suits Helga so well that when I asked her about disadvantages she could not think of any! For her there have not been any difficulties. However, she is aware that this way of working might not suit everyone.

I suppose it really depends on the situation you're in. I mean for me it's worked out very well. But I think that, for anyone, having the option of two jobs means you've more job security. I think if someone has the opportunity to get two part-time jobs then I'd say have a go and see what you think.

Think about the hidden opportunities which may exist. If the in-work benefits are the same for a part-timer as a full-timer, then I'd say that having a collection of part-time jobs is something to consider.

> I've worked full-time (before I had the children) and I've also had just one part-time job – and now two part-time jobs, so I've had the experience of all three, and I still think I'd go for two part-time jobs.

Helga has managed to find two posts which, for her, perfectly balance each other. She has managed to avoid the problems created by having to do too much travelling between the two places of work and her home, minimizing the sort of strains and expense which Ali experienced.

Portfolio working is obviously not a cure-all for everyone. As with most situations there are pros and cons. It is worth while summarizing a few of the points raised for you to bear in mind before deciding whether you want to 'go portfolio'.

The Pros

'. . . statistics indicate that your greatest chance of working in the future is to ensure that you are working in the present . . .' (*Part-time Work*, Judith Humphries).

- Your everlasting (but seemingly unreachable?) dream may be to work full-time. However, it may be worth considering working even part-time in your chosen field in order to stand a better chance of stepping into the core of full-time workers. It happened for Ali; it could happen for you. And, like him, a second job could be taken simply for the financial advantage it provides; or you could even find yourself working in your chosen field but with more than one employer. Portfolio working can give you an alternative full-time solution.
- You will be enlarging your contacts with people. This may benefit you both socially and professionally. Being in the right place at the right time to hear about full-time jobs before they are advertised is often how vacancies are filled – that is, if you still want a full-time job.
- You will be entering a growing market. As we have seen, part-

time jobs are on the increase – which means you have a wider choice.

- Having more than one job improves your overall job security. If one of them disappears, it does not mean all of them disappear, as is the case with full-time work. Think of it as giving yourself more baskets in which to put your eggs!
- You have the chance to organize your working timetable to suit your preferences and other commitments.
- It enables you to gain a wide range of experience; and if you want to toe-dip and find out what it is like to work in a particular environment, you can more easily do so without jeopardizing your total job security should it not work out.
- Work fulfils many functions: social, financial, developmental and so on. It is rare to find one job which is able to fulfil all, just as it is rare for one relationship to serve all our many complex personal needs. Having more than one job increases the chance of your experience of work being a fulfilling one.
- Elements of your personal portfolio can be changed as your tastes and needs change and develop – without causing a crisis.
- There may be financial gains to be made. For example, in the UK no Social Security deductions are made from the first portion of any wage you earn. If you have one job you have only one 'free' portion; if you have two jobs, you have two 'free' portions. Check out beforehand what the tax and benefits situation is. You may end up better off than you think.
- As Helga points out, the enjoyment to be gained from the variety of two (or more) jobs is not to be underestimated. I too work portfolio. Besides writing (my main activity) I also work for a local employment project – an excellent counterpoint to the more solitary work of being an author.

The Cons

To balance up the picture, the potential disadvantages also have to be considered. Some are related to being engaged in part-time work; some to having a portfolio:

- In some countries part-time workers receive fewer benefits than their full-time counterparts. This may include loss of holiday entitlement, health cover, pensions, production bonuses, staff discounts and overtime rates.
- Because the part-time workforce has been gaining in strength only relatively recently, and in a time of high unemployment, employers in some areas where legislation is lax may have an exploitative attitude towards pay and conditions.
- You can feel less part of the office life as a part-timer and miss out on vital communication and meetings.
- Core staff can have a different attitude to part-timers. They do not expect them to want to be involved. This is fine with some part-timers, but if you want to be involved and find that your opinions are not sought out along with everyone else's, you can feel like an outsider.
- Working part-time may still carry its own negativity on a CV in the eyes of less enlightened employers (in which case, would you want to work for them?)
- You may find yourself overlooked when training sessions are planned and when promotion opportunities arise, although this depends on the legislation of the country in which you work.
- If the jobs in your portfolio do not gel well you might find yourself dashing around from job to job without enough time to switch mentally from one to the other.

Making It Work

Although there are potential pitfalls, there are also strategies to adopt which may help:

- *Know your rights.* These do vary from country to country, and as governments become more keen to promote part-time work legislation is changing rapidly. Find out what benefits you are entitled to, what financial incentives you may be able to claim, and what your legal in-work entitlements are.

- *Weigh up the travelling costs and time before committing yourself to any particular part-time job.* Consider the likelihood of being able to find a second or third job to make up your portfolio in the same neighbourhood or part of town as your first job. Grouping them together will make your portfolio more workable. If they cannot be in the same area, having at least one near your home will help.
- *If travelling is involved, arrange to do full days where possible in each area.* This will cut down on your travel expenses.
- *Consider your other commitments and how well they will fit into the new picture.*
- *Consider whether the dress codes for the different jobs are compatible.*
- *Depending on the company benefits and statutory entitlements, you might need to consider making other arrangements to cover you for sick leave, holidays and pensions.*
- *Ask about on-the-job training.* If it is unlikely that you will be included you may have to become your own Human Resources Manager and consider making your own arrangements to enable you to keep ahead of developments in your field(s). However, employers may be happy to make arrangements once they understand your commitment to your work – despite being part-time.
- *If legislation where you live and work does not oblige your employers to inform you of promotion opportunities or other vacancies, you may have to push yourself forward and let them know you want to be kept informed.*
- *Familiarize yourself with the communication routes in your different places of work.* Find out how information is distributed – and ensure you receive it all. Identify where the noticeboards are and make sure you check them regularly. It might be an idea to link up with someone who works an alternative part-time rota, or with a core worker, and get him or her to swap gossip/vital info/new developments with you. Start to build your own in-work networks.
- *With any part-time work it is easy to feel as though you must prove your worth, and so end up putting in extra work.* Establish the

boundaries early on with colleagues, line managers – and yourself.

- *Join a union.* Part-timers can be in a more vulnerable position than full-time members of staff, especially if you are in the minority.
- *Consider the relative merits of working for small and large organizations.* Larger ones may have better developed systems for managing part-time workers, but smaller companies can be more flexible.

In what has been a difficult time for unemployed people in many industrialized countries it is good to see that there is one area which is growing and which offers opportunities. Portfolio work is still a new idea to many and may not suit all people. However, the benefits of being able to remain in the job market and combine a number of job interests is now becoming an acceptable way in which to steer one's career. With governments and businesses keen to promote part-time working, perhaps it will not be long before part-timers are more evenly spread throughout the different strata of the workforce, and treated just as well as their full-time counterparts. In fact, as businesses realize their worth, employers may eventually see that they must learn to value part-time workers if they are to attract and retain the staff they need.

CHAPTER THREE

Short-term Contract Work

Before recent times, when someone applied for a job it was with the justified assumption that, if successful, they would be taking up the post for an indefinite period. Things have changed.

What do we find now when we look at job ads? What are all these tagged-on stipulations about 'duration' buried deep in an increasing number of advertisements? 'The post will be for three months.' 'The contract will be for one year in the first instance.' 'Wanted. For six months.' One suddenly realizes one has to be eagle-eyed about these things. I mean to say, you do not want to end up with a job for just half a year now, do you? Anyway, it cannot be a *real* job – or can it?

Traditionally, temporary work has been seen as an area for those who are not serious about having a career, or who are perhaps not even too serious about work at all. 'Temping' is well known in most countries and conjures up images of typists, filling in for so-and-so who has come down with the flu. It has also been associated with 'casual' work in seasonal jobs such as those in agriculture, tourism and so on. Certainly it has mainly been thought of in terms of unskilled or semi-skilled work and has carried with it a certain low-key stigma.

But times are changing.

What Is Contract Work?

Short-term contract work is not temping. Neither is it sub-contracting, nor consultancy work.

Temping, or temporary work, tends to be open-ended and for a short term; perhaps for only a day or even half a day. The work tends to be in lower-grade jobs which carry few responsibilities. As a rule, assignments involve just one individual being taken on by a business or department on an occasional basis, as opposed to a group being hired as part of a planned exercise.

Sub-contract work, now often called 'outsourcing', refers to the practice whereby businesses buy in another company's ability to deliver a service. Sub-contract work can be carried out on the sub-contractor's own premises or at the contractor's place of work. Sub-contract work is invoiced for payment, just as the delivery of goods is, but in this case a service is being delivered instead. Examples of sub-contract work include catering, cleaning, security and delivery services.

Consultancy work is a bit like sub-contracting. Consultants tend to be self-employed and invoice for the work they carry out. It is different from the work of someone on a short-term contract in that consultants are brought in to assess a situation and recommend a course of action.

Short-term contract work involves workers in specific undertakings. Short-term contract workers, by and large, carry out duties or tasks specified by the employer. They are employed by the company with whom they have the contract and are on their payroll. Assignments are longer than one would normally expect with temporary work; taking people on with short-term contracts is usually part of a planned exercise by an employer.

The Changing Picture

Previously, any non-permanent staff have been used by employers for understandable reasons: to cover staff absences, when

29

additional 'hands' are needed for a special event or to help with a rushed order, and so on. But short-term contract work is now coming into its own as employers see its potential as another tool to enhance the numerical flexibility of its workforce.

As before, a business needs to be able to respond to the expansion and contraction of its workload, but the recession has made it even more imperative if companies are to remain competitive. Competitiveness means cutting unnecessary overheads and bringing in essential staff when and only when needed, which cuts the cost of retaining expensive permanent staff. Hiring staff on short-term contracts is cheaper for businesses. Some may not be able to afford, on a permanent basis, the high calibre of staff needed only occasionally, such as in-house accountants.

Many organizations, both public and private, have undergone massive internal changes during the recession. At periods like this it can be difficult, if not impossible, for future staffing levels to be predicted much beyond the next few months. Employing people on short-term contracts is one way in which many companies have coped with the situation.

The use of contract workers often comes down to the economics of the situation – it helps employers save money. But there are other factors which have attracted further interest in this method of staffing.

Funding redundancy payments can inflict high costs on a business which may already be struggling to survive in challenging economic times. Depending on where you live, only permanent members of staff are eligible for such payments, and then only after a qualifying period. By recruiting staff on shorter term contracts an employer can cut its provision for redundancy payments, should they be needed. And since unemployment is high in many countries, for employers there has been the added bonus of a ready pool of available people to attract with vacancies offering short-term contract work.

The increase in the number of women in the workforce has also had its effect, especially as they are now a valuable commodity helping to fill the recruitment gap brought about by a drop in the number of school leavers as the 'baby boom' generations fade away. Companies have had to adopt more suitable working arrangements to accommodate maternity leave; if they wish to retain female staff with valuable skills and expertise they must arrange maternity cover, often via a contract worker. The same applies when companies introduce other flexible working arrangements, such as parental leave, career breaks, sabbaticals and study leave, or enable parents to work on a term-time-only basis. Cover has to be found for all these situations.

In order to establish a more dependable peripheral workforce, some larger organizations have introduced *zero contracts*. This means that short-listed people are interviewed and offered a contract but with no guarantee of any minimum hours. This on-call arrangement gives the employer maximum flexibility with minimum (even non-existent) commitment, without having to resort to using temping agencies – and paying the fees they charge.

The number of employees taking part in short-term contract work varies from country to country although employers are beginning to consider increasing their use of it, if they have not done so already. For example, only 5 per cent of employees are temporary workers in Belgium, while Spain has the highest number at over 30 per cent. While we have mentioned the commercial reasons why employers use contract workers, legislation in each country also has an effect on its use and popularity. In some countries contract work is tightly regulated, such as in Luxembourg where two years is the maximum for contracts, including renewals. By contrast, in the UK, Irish Republic and Denmark there are no restrictions on their use.

Financial incentives offered by some governments to employers (in France and Spain, for example) in order to help reduce unemployment levels have also had an impact on the increased use of short-term contracts. Of course legislation can change at any time, but like businesses, governments are realizing that by promoting flexible working arrangements they too can score 'brownie points' by taking measures which seem to reduce the numbers of people unemployed.

Because of all these changes, the profile of contract workers is also changing. No longer is it an area dominated by unskilled women, as has been the case in the past. Both male and female, unskilled and professional are being brought into this section of the job market. In spring 1994, figures from the Labour Force Survey in the UK showed that men are still lagging behind and holding on to the job-for-life idea. Of those in temporary work, half were there as a second option; they had wanted a permanent job, whereas this applied to only a third of women. However, one in five men had made a positive choice to take contract work; still not up to the one in three women, but the numbers are growing. Overall, non-permanent work increased by a marked 10 per cent over the year, with the majority of both men and women being on contract (as opposed to temping through an agency, which accounted for only 8 per cent of all non-permanent work).

The Short-term Contract Experience

For many of us, taking on a job for only a limited period is an alien concept. We have grown use to staying in a post until we decide to leave, which might in the end be after only nine months but which might equally be after nine years, or more. To take on a job for a set time-span seems so limiting somehow; so finite. It seems as though our sense of security is having a time-limit placed on it. Yet we must face the fact that job security does not really exist for any of us anymore. With successive waves of redundancies we have to accept the awful truth that job security was in fact a facade. Faced with this realization, could we perhaps come around to thinking that a guarantee of a job for one year may well have its advantages? At least we are secure for a full 12 months. But what will it be like if we decide to take the plunge?

I talked to Zena about her experience of working on short-term contracts. She works in education – previously seen as a secure and traditional environment in which to be employed. But now things are very different. How has she coped?

I work as a tutor at a college in London with students who have special educational needs. I also teach in the evening at

32

another college as well. They're both short-term contracts going from year to year.

The culture of short-term contracts has come about in this college because it wants to save money, you see, so they don't appoint full-time permanent staff with lots of rights when really they might have to start cutting back. So instead of them looking at ways to raise money they're cutting back.

I used to have a permanent job but, like a lot of people, I was made redundant. After that happened I got some part-time work in the library through a contact at the college and then I started meeting different people. They found out I was a qualified teacher and also trained in producing educational media, and someone said 'We're looking for someone like you in the Special Needs department,' so I was told to send in a CV. I had an interview and I was given some part-time work for the department, teaching English. That contract was for a term.

For the first year I had contracts for a term at a time, but at times I'd get extra odd hours put on, depending on the need, and so I'd get extra odd contracts for creating learning materials, paid for out of a special budget. I also got some contracts from a commercial organization to create some specialist learning materials.

It has all evolved from taking that first term's contract in the library. They had some money available and they needed someone to input some database material. They usually used agency people but this person knew I was looking for work and that I could do it, so she asked me if I was interested.

Then it developed into termly contracts over a period of about 18 months to two years, but then the termly contracts became too much in that I was doing over the hours I was supposed to. Eventually I had to stop my contracts and what happened then was the Personnel Department allowed me to invoice them for the extra hours – like a self-employed person. Some of the money was coming from one source of funding and I was allowed to treat that as a private job and to invoice them for it – but that was exceptional.

One of my bosses fought to get me a 0.8 job for a year on the understanding that a lot of it was to be co-ordinating learning support and some other work. They really did have to fight for it. Then after they'd appointed me they found they hadn't got the money – but I'd got an agreement so they couldn't renege on it. I was very lucky. I mean, the work is there and there is no way my Head of Special Needs could have fitted it in with her workload as well.

Working on short-term contracts can put you in a vulnerable position. Goodness knows what's going to happen next year because I've only been given a year's contract. I probably won't find out about whether it is going to be renewed or not until the very last minute; it's always last minute. They say 'Well, go ahead and start work,' but you haven't got a contract in your hand and that's how the complications came about before when I ended up doing too many hours; I'd already done half of them when they pulled the plug.

It's very common, this sort of thing in the college. They're trying to get heads of department to give out contracts immediately, but with their workloads they never do. There is meant to be some redress if they don't; you're meant to be able to go to the principal and let them know straight away if there are problems. That's the idea, but you're not going to, are you? You're too busy getting on with the work, and if you land the heads of department in it, that's it, isn't it? – you're saying they're not doing their job. Their workloads are so massive as well, it's just too enormous for too few people.

The lack of dependability on the contracts, plus the newness of the culture to the organization she is working for are adding certain strains to Zena's position. These may be less apparent if someone were to work for a company which had more clear-cut operational guidelines and where managers were more adept at coping with the demands of contract staff.

Despite these difficulties Zena does have this to say about what it is like to work in this way:

One benefit is the varied work, plus if you're available you're free to do other freelance work, so you can take advantage of any other opportunities which come up. And I also notice that if you've done a good job you'll be asked to do some more work, which is what you don't get in full-time work. You get a much more immediate feedback of appreciation of what you've done, which in full-time jobs goes by the by these days. But there are practical disadvantages. Here in the UK you don't get sick pay; you can't have leave when you like (but you can't in education very much anyway); you're not paid during holiday times unless you're on a year's contract, but not with termly contracts; and no pensions or anything like that.

So although you're there practically as a full-time, permanent member of staff you're not getting any of the benefits. Your pay isn't any higher even though you are working under similar circumstances to a 'freelance', who is normally better paid. You're just paid *pro rata*, so I've lost out by being put on to an 0.8. On a termly contract you do get paid a slightly higher rate. As an 0.8 I'm falling between two stools. And if I end up in the summer having no work, or at Easter having no work . . . When I was on the termly contract it meant I could sign on and get housing benefit and sometimes unemployment benefit, but now I can't and I'm only on the same pay – in fact a little less.

So to make up the shortfalls in my income I've just got lots of other part-time jobs. I work at the other college some evenings, do odd bits of theatre work, odd bits of design work, all sorts of odd things. Anything which comes my way and I can fit in, I'll do.

This is obviously very different from Zena's previous situation, where the work was regular and she did not have the responsibility of having to make her own provision for things like pensions. These demands have affected her in various ways.

It changes your character. You become more forthright. If you're looking for work you go up and tell people, 'Look,

I'm looking for extra hours.' You become much more up front about things and say what you mean. And you definitely become more confident because you're having to push yourself forward more.

You've always got your ears to the ground trying to find work. I suppose in that way it makes you more outgoing in that you're looking in all sorts of places for work so it widens your horizons. When you're in full-time work you can just get in a rut, a sort of pattern.

But whether it's leading me away from or towards my life's aims . . . I'd say it's leading me all over the place! I suppose I have lost focus on what I really want to do. I love creating learning materials but I've become a tutor, which is not what I really wanted to do. So I'm waiting for the right thing to come along, although I'm tending not to make the time to look for those full-time jobs. I find it really difficult every week to look through the papers and properly look for a job.

But all in all I think it's definitely worth doing if you're going to be gaining skills or it's in a company which could lead to other work – which is what happened in my case. I found there was work all over the place which I wouldn't have known about otherwise. I think you can definitely pick up other work. If they like you they may keep you on for a few more weeks or they might tell you about another job coming up in another department.

I also try and learn as much as possible from each situation. All the time your skills are being increased. Yes – be pushy in that way and do other things. And always have your eye on the next thing. It has to be that way. Keep one step ahead. It's like being self-employed in that respect. I know contracts get renewed and renewed and renewed, but it can lull you into a false sense of security. I think you've always got to keep that in the back of your mind and keep things in the pipeline; I know some people who have worked for years on short-term contracts and suddenly it has ended and they've been devastated. It's because they lost sight that it only ever was a short-term contract – you can't rely on it for permanence.

Variety of work is the main thing which keeps me there, and plus in education it is well paid for what it is. With short-term contracts you've got to be sure you're not going to be out of pocket; you do have to work out the financial side of it.

I also think you have to be suited to it. I think there are some people who couldn't cope with it. You have to be quite level-headed and determined. You have so many things on the go – it's like being self-employed. I try to keep my eyes on the jobs, but it all depends. If I'm up to my eyes in work I may not look at a paper for two months, but I do have friends who are looking out for me as well, who'll give me a ring and say, 'Hey, have you seen this?' so that's quite helpful. Networking – that's really one of the most important things. In fact it's vital.

So, Zena thinks not everyone would be suited to it. As with part-time work, short-term contracting is not a universal cure-all for everybody's employment difficulties. But to help you decide whether it may be for you or not, let us look at a summary of some of the pros and cons:

The Pros

- In conversation, Zena mentioned a number of times how much she enjoyed the variety which this new situation provided; variety which might be difficult to find in a regular, permanent job.
- There appears to be a greater element of challenge to handling this sort of situation, which some people may relish.
- You may find your work more appreciated, especially on the shorter-term contracts, which could give you more job satisfaction.
- It provides you with the opportunity to experience a range of different work environments.
- It can provide you with a way in which either to take on more work or ease off from having a permanent workload.

- It can be an opportunity in which to both develop and extend your skills.
- In many countries (such as France, Spain and the UK) this is one of the growing areas in the job market.
- As more companies adopt flexible working arrangements, the status of people on short-term contracts is improving.
- It enables you to choose when you want to work.
- Once you have your foot in the door with a company you are in a position to prove yourself. You are also in a good position to apply for other posts when they come up, whether they be other contracts or permanent posts.
- Contracts can often be extended or renewed, although an employer's ability to do so depends on the legislation in each country. For example, in Belgium if two contracts are run on consecutively it is deemed to represent an open-ended contract, which some employers might be unwilling to accept. In Germany, 18 months is the maximum term for a contract. In the UK and some other countries the situation is very different, with no limits placed on the duration, extension or renewal of contracts by employers.
- Once you become settled in operating as a contract worker you may start to feel increasingly comfortable with selecting the kinds of jobs you want to take on board. You can always say 'No' to a contract – and 'Yes' to ones which particularly appeal to you.
- Through changing your workplace regularly you will inevitably extend your range of both social and professional contacts, making networking more effective.
- In some countries you may be eligible for an end-of-contract bonus, as well as having a high level of protection of your rights, such as in France.
- Depending on the company, and where you live, you may receive a higher rate of pay than permanent staff, as was the case with Zena when she was on an academic termly contract.
- It can help develop aspects of your character. Zena has found it has increased her confidence and made her more forthright.
- With careful planning, it can lead you towards your work/career/life goals.

The Cons

Some of the disadvantages hinge on the statutory regulations governing non-permanent workers; others relate to the situation itself:

- If you work in the UK, Irish Republic or the US, for example, your rights are not automatically the same as those for core staff, although some fringe benefits might be included in your contract, depending on the company.
- You may have gaps between when one contract ends and another begins.
- Should you need them, your entitlement to out-of-work benefits may be affected by working on short-term contracts or by taking on a zero-hours contract. This depends on where you live.
- There is little likelihood of promotion within the bounds of a contract, so if the contract is for, say, two years you will be working at the same level for that period of time without the opportunity for progression up the scale. There will obviously be exceptions to this.
- As a non-permanent member of staff you may feel vulnerable to shifts in company policy, etc.
- A working life based on short-term contracts demands a great deal of initiative. As Zena points out, you have to be more pushy about finding work, which may not suit everybody.
- Renewed contracts may lead you to a false sense of security.
- Staff attitudes may be different towards you because you are not part of the core contingent, although this may change as flexible arrangements become more commonly accepted.

Making It Work

It may feel as though you will have to make a big shift in order to turn your previous *modus operandi* around and consider taking on work which has a limited shelf-life. This is not what the majority of us have been taught to expect from our work, and it can appear to be a very insecure way of working. Here are some pointers to help you make it work:

- *Know your rights.* These differ from country to country. You may end up better paid, or be able to look forward to end-of-contract bonuses, but unless you know your rights and entitlements you will be less able to make a decision which is right for you, or to make contingency plans to offset any gaps in statutory provision and entitlements. This may include deciding to take out a personal pension or your own health insurance.
- *Plan your yearly work requirements to reflect your financial needs, holiday plans and other commitments.*
- *You need to be adaptable, responsive, willing to learn and able to fit in easily to new situations.* Think about whether you have the necessary qualities.
- *At interviews, find out to which company fringe benefits you would be entitled.*
- *Ensure that the funding of your contract is securely in place.* This may be of more concern when applying for posts with non-commercial organizations.
- *Get any agreement in writing* before *you start work.*
- *At interviews, check how developed the systems are for managing staff on short-term contracts.* At Zena's college her line managers seemed to be learning as they went along, which eventually caused her difficulties.
- *If your contract is to cover someone's absence, find out if there will be a cross-over period, or whether one can be arranged.* You do not want to be wading in to sort out someone else's mess.
- *Non-permanent staff can be excluded from in-house training programmes.* If so, you might have to consider developing your own training programme and integrating it into your working year. Government grants or loans may be available to help you do this.
- *Establish the periods of notice, and if possible, try to negotiate as long a one as possible in your favour.*

40

- *Plan beforehand for positive use of any gaps which may occur between contracts.* You might plan to use the time for training, travel, domestic duties – or simply for reflection and reassessment.

- *Consider having a zero-hours contract in place for you to use as a fall-back should you unexpectedly end up between contracts.* There may be employment agencies in your area which specialize in placing people on contract (as opposed to temporary) work. Check them out. Think about what other fall-back positions you could put in place in order to develop your own security net. The more eggs you have in this particular safety basket the better. Remember it is always easier to turn down work than to start scrabbling around at the last minute to find some, but do keep recruiters informed if you take up a contract which will keep you out of commission for any length of time. They will probably appreciate you keeping them informed.

Perhaps the most important aspect to successful short-term working is always to keep your eye on the ball, on the next job, on lining up the next contract. As Zena points out, developing a network is an essential tool in helping to maximize the number of opportunities you hear about. Do build in regular time to plan ahead and look at what your next work-related goal might be. Although the opportunity for promotion within a contract is limited, there is no reason why each successive contract should not take you further up the ladder towards the promotional level you might be after. And despite being employed, you have to become an entrepreneur, keeping your ear to the ground and watching out for the next opportunity – or learning how to create it yourself.

Short-term contract work might not be for everyone, but if you are able to learn how to keep the ball rolling it may offer you a more secure way of working and a lot more variety, which may certainly be far more enjoyable than what's available in a regular nine-to-five job.

CHAPTER FOUR

Teleworking

Although many of the new flexible work arrangements are developments or extensions of existing work practices, teleworking is a completely new phenomenon.

What Does It Mean?

This new way of working involves the use of telecommunications technology at a location which is remote from the employer's own base or premises. Equipment is used to carry out the work tasks as well as communicate with customers, clients, line managers, suppliers, colleagues or staff.

The remote location may be your own home or it may be a nearby 'satellite office' called a *telecentre*. Self-employed people might use a *telecottage* – a local centre set up for use by those whose business involves teleworking. Some teleworkers are mobile, using portable equipment in cars or hotel rooms to carry out their work.

Although you may telework alone at home, you could be organized by your employer into a project team or group with which you communicate electronically – as well as by the more conventional telephone.

The hard and fast definition of a teleworker varies from country to country. In the Netherlands the official body Netherlands

Telework Platform (PTN) defines it as work of which at least 20 per cent is carried out away from the organization's main base, using information and communications technology. This contrasts with the UK, for example, where one report cites a figure of least 50 per cent.

An agreed core definition may be yet to come, but teleworking itself is already here.

How It Has Developed

It goes without saying that teleworking has come about through the development of new technology. Besides the major advances in the sophistication of personal computers, adaptations of commercial equipment for the home market have also made an impact. Fax machines, photocopiers, modems (to enable computers to connect to on-line systems and allow people to communicate with each other via their computers) and advanced computer printers have all had their part to play, as has the mush-rooming emergence of highly sophisticated software.

Further afield, the development of optical fibres and the computerization of telephone exchanges has facilitated the transmission of data from one point of communication to another, be that via a fax machine or computer.

And as the latest technology comes on-stream, new facilities become available to computer users everywhere: teleconferencing (via computers), video conferencing (via televisions) and telephone conferencing. The international dimension has been added with developments in the technology of space satellites.

But technology alone has not been responsible for the development of teleworking. A whole diverse range of factors appears to have conjoined and influenced the picture. For example, in the US a change in the legislation on pollution has put an obligation on employers in some key cities to cut the amount of commuting their employees must do. In response, some employers have considered teleworking. In Holland, teleworking is being positively promoted via the PTN to businesses, but in Japan it is less popular although the Japanese have shown an interest in telecentres and telecottages.

For businesses, teleworking provides another way in which to increase competitiveness. Having staff work away from the main office for part (if not all) of the time brings major savings on overheads. Capital need no longer be tied up in expensive commercial properties; costs associated with its maintenance decline; providing facilities for on-site staff becomes unnecessary. Normally, a building's productive use may be below 5 per cent, according to the FI Group in the UK, which makes providing space for on-site workers an expensive business.

Many businesses are also realizing that they can utilize another form of outsourcing if teleworkers become self-employed. For example, Rank Xerox has assisted some employees in setting up as independent contractors to whom the company then subcontracts its work. This cuts down employment overheads even more for the parent company.

Teleworking at home has obvious appeal to many parents who wish to combine work with being involved in child-care activities. For companies who have been keen to recruit and retain women with very marketable IT skills, introducing teleworking as an option has enabled this to take place.

In the past, any form of homeworking has tended to be associated with low-status work, but many businesses are realizing that a number of their executives are able to manage their workloads from home for at least part of the time, providing they have the necessary technology to enable them to do so. Charles Handy in his book *The Age of Unreason* writes, 'What is new is the higher skills, qualifications and status of the new homeworkers.' Many of this new breed in the UK are top wage earners.

Another aspect is that as businesses become part of the global market, teleworking enables work to be imported and exported from country to country via telecommunications technology, as managers go in search of the most highly competitive rates.

So, work for a London company can now be carried out by teleworkers in India; and skills and tasks can be carried out by workers in other time zones around the world to make a more cost-effective 24-hour operation now possible.

As teleworking becomes established research studies are beginning to confirm its effectiveness for businesses. Increases in productivity, normally lost at the organization's main place of work through interruptions, chatting with colleagues and coffee-breaks, are estimated to be between 40 and 50 per cent. This has serious implications for companies far and wide in addressing the problem of how to maintain or improve their profitability.

Already in the US, 8 per cent of the workforce is teleworking. In the UK a prediction of over 10 million teleworkers by the year 2001 has been suggested by the Henley Centre for Forecasting as businesses continue their downsizing exercises. And a Europe-wide study conducted by the German research company Empirica in 1994 reported that in the UK there were already 7.4 per cent of the workforce teleworking, 7 per cent in France, 4.8 per cent in Germany and 3.6 per cent in Spain.

Some teleworkers work at home for only part of the working week, the rest spent 'back at head office'. Telecentres are helping to answer the needs of those who prefer to keep in real, as opposed to virtual, contact with colleagues.

Francis Kinsman, the futurist guru, believes teleworking will be one of the great growth areas, evenly split between the employed and self-employed, although he also believes it will not be popular with younger people, who often want to be out of the home to socialize as much as possible. He sees many teleworking jobs waiting to be discovered with the introduction of future generations of technology.

It seems that we are coming full circle, back to how most people used to work – that is, from home, with the exception that the path to bringing in the bread now leads down the telephone wire.

The Teleworking Experience

The Employer

I talked to one employer, Thomas, about teleworking and what it has meant to him and his company, to see whether research reports match reality:

My wife and I set up a consultancy in IT in 1988. Really our determination was to set up a company that required virtually no people and used as much technology as possible, so to do this we set up from home and expanded from there, although in terms of space we haven't expanded beyond the room. We use technology wherever we can.

It's not just the two of us in the company. It's just the two of us here. We've got some 30 consultants, most of whom work from home. They vary from being ex-IT managers, directors of companies, ex-marketing directors, senior people, retired people. They have a lot of experience there, rather than the normal consultants who, while very bright and clever, lack experience. We cover the whole spectrum of disciplines from promotion to quality management to marketing plans and developing equipment, etc., even setting up venture capital for people. It's all related to companies involved with IT.

Our consultants are spread all over the country, but by using electronic mail (e-mail) it's just as though you were in an office next door. I also use a remote secretarial service where we can either fax or dictate over the phone from wherever we are and the typed letters come back on e-mail on our preferred word processors; it works like that for everyone in our network. This service even sends faxes for us, so it takes a lot of aggravation away. We also use a reception service which fields all our calls, and diverts them as necessary. We have the telephone on 'Permanent' or 'Divert, I'm busy', and they answer in the name of our company and take messages. It works brilliantly. It allows us to break through the problem of having to be near our markets and of living in a location where transport is a problem.

In the last year or two outsourcing has become an OK phrase, and because of that teleworking is being viewed now as a form of outsourcing and it's actually starting to happen.

Technology provides you with so many things which you needed people to do before. Filing papers is all done electronically. I've become proficient as a four-fingered typist where before I wouldn't think of touching a keyboard because I would have made lots of errors. They didn't have spell-checkers then. The accounting system used to be a department, but the software is so good now that it doesn't take a second to raise an invoice, and you don't need loads of printouts because it's all on the system for the auditor at the end of the year. There's just a little bit of filing of receipts and things like that which you can't get away from wherever you are.

I'm growing, finding ways of growing the business. There are certain businesses you can't run on this basis. Distribution businesses require space. There are things you can't do with teleworking.

You can still find companies which are set up like little empires. I don't think they will ever disappear but I do think that the virtual company where people are employed by say two or three companies for their work will come about. Consultancies which are eye-ball to eye-ball will continue to happen – you can't get away from that and I wouldn't want to – but I think there's a real sea-change happening because of technology and because of the need to have greater flexibility. We've even got members on our network outside the UK because teleworking doesn't have national barriers. We have one member in America.

As for the future of our business, it will develop as technology develops and I suppose we will grow the number of outworkers. With new integrated digital services coming on line it will be easier to link people together so that we all have the one telephone number, so that the only difference from us working in an office is that we don't have doors. In fact that's an extremely inefficient way of running a business, with all those overheads, as well as all the interruptions you get to your work. You want to sit down and write and then the phone goes and your train of thought goes with it.

Teleworking might appeal to people who are looking for an option that is flexible enough to enable them to work from home. Thomas again:

My advice for anyone thinking about a career in teleworking would be, don't think you can start at the age of 18. You've got to have experience of business before you can do that. I would say two to three years as an accountant or secretary or whatever, so you can pick up the disciplines of business. Then you can go and telework.

I think eventually people will be able to develop these skills at school before they actually go out to work as such, and education will be much more aligned to the next stage in the development of work. I think teleworking will also give people greater opportunities, not only for accountants and such, but archaeologists, programmers, systems analysts, etc. All these people will be able to do their work from home. I think it gives one wonderful freedom.

If you're thinking of setting up independently as a tele-worker, I'd say the first thing is to join an association like the National Association of Teleworkers here in the UK, only because it has its concentration focused on teleworking.

I'd also say to use as much technology as possible. You can rent it. You don't have to pour out lots of shekels, but don't get too focused on the technology. Keep your focus on the job. It's easy with computers to get hooked on wonderful little packages. Also, companies must look at teleworking as a very cost-effective way of performing services.

One thing I learned is that I need four telephone lines: one each for data, fax, private use and a business line. If you try and have one of these tele/fax switches you can't really run a business. It defiles any image you're trying to set up in that it says 'Hey, this is someone working from home with a funny fax switch.' Here there is someone answering with the name of the company and so on. You've got to set up properly.

We've a scanner for taking information from hard copy into the system. It works so brilliantly and I don't know what we'd do without one. We have three printers set up with different stationery, so you can switch automatically to and from your word processor. Unfortunately there's no one telling teleworkers how to telework.

The Employee

But what is it like to work for an employer as a teleworker? Terri is in her early forties, married with one child. Teleworking has been her one and only career. She has seen it develop from its initial stages – indeed she must have been one of the first:

I was teleworking before it was teleworking – 1975. I was a technical author with one of the computer giants; in fact I'd been working there for 18 months and at that time they had a scheme for working remotely from the office. So when we moved down here to this rural area in the southwest of the country I brought my job down here. Initially that was on a self-employed basis but the Social Security people caught up with the company over it because in fact we were employed, not self-employed, so after a couple of years I went back to employed status. From the practical point of view you could say it was a continuation of work, but back then the teleworking idea was completely new. It was seen as a way of keeping hold of women who were leaving to have babies. There was a problem at the beginning of the 1970s in that they'd got a lot of women who had started programming. It was a very young industry at that time – you wouldn't see anyone over 40 in the corridors, so that meant that all these women were leaving together to have babies. So the teleworking idea really was new when I started.

I progressed in my teleworking job to the point where I

was managing a team of 13 at one stage while my colleague was on maternity leave. I was project managing; team managing off-site staff anyway.

You could say I don't know how to work in an office. I only worked 18 months on site, so my entire career really has been teleworking.

The benefits for me of teleworking have varied over the years, as you can appreciate. The initial benefit was obviously being able to make the move down here. We had wanted to move down for domestic reasons; my father-in-law died and so we moved down to his smallholding, and so teleworking made that possible, otherwise we would have found it quite difficult to come down here. So that was the first thing, that we were able to move somewhere where there weren't the jobs in the locality, not in the career that I wanted.

Then there's the advantage of flexi-work. When I first came down here I didn't work full-time because I was trying to help run the smallholding as a business.

In theory teleworking should have been worse in terms of career progression, but I was certainly well paid. There were a lot of women who were actually in the process of having their babies, so the whole remote-working scheme grew a lot; the technical authoring side grew a lot, too. We also had an in-house contract system that sold services to another part of the company; when that was set up I became project manager.

I suppose if I'd been on-site I would have found some equivalent, or something or other would have happened and I would have progressed my career. It certainly didn't do any harm teleworking, but I was in the right place at the right time to make quite a rapid progression at that stage.

It also meant I could have my child without any apparently major changes in working practices.

On the personal side there is the freedom which that flexibility brings you. When we were first down here as young marrieds if we wanted to go shopping on an afternoon then we could go mid-week. You could trade time across, so it was very good from that point of view, although it's had its moments – there were times when it put an extra strain on the relationship but that could be true of any – I mean, we've been married for 20 years. I wouldn't say it was a problem or that it caused any particular difficulties. On balance I'd say it was an advantage.

The Down Side

So, is there a down side to teleworking? If you can no longer depend on the automatic extension of your social life which working in an office or other place of work brings, what are the consequences? Terri:

We don't have a particularly active social life. It's mostly centred around having a child and living in a village, so we've got involved in a few things there; the playgroup, and getting to know other families and so on with children of the same age who can do things together. The advantages accrue for all women who stay at home with their children. They build a social network within their local community, but with us it has probably been there for both of us. But I haven't made a special effort.

There is the business of separating the domestic and business work, which can be quite difficult. When I worked for the company [Terri is now self-employed and runs her own teleworking business] I had hours of work for the week and I kept a running total of the hours I was working. I didn't necessarily work the same number of hours a day. You might sit down to work and then think 'I'm not going to do this now, I'm going to do some gardening, and then I can do it this evening, or whatever.' It's easier for people in an office or more traditional job, who can say 'Well, I've done my hours this week and that's the end of it.' Equally it can be that much more difficult to leave domestic problems behind. If there's something very pressing you have to stop work and deal with it. If you were at work you'd be away from it and would not have to deal with it until you came home. So it can be more difficult to separate the two and to some extent you have to accept this. I guess it suits people with more workaholic tendencies.

I would point out that if you work because you have to and don't really enjoy what you're doing, then doing it at home is certainly *not* going to be that easy one way or another, for all sorts of reasons. I think probably you have to like what you're doing, in which case the fact that you're working in the evening or whatever is neither here nor there, and probably no different from taking work home from the office. Teleworking certainly makes work a lot easier to manage. At least if I pop upstairs to do an extra couple of hours work, I'm not saying 'I have to go to the office on Sunday.' It's a real wrecker that one, isn't it?

In terms of feeling left out of what was going on at the office, I normally didn't, but various reorganizations began before I left and the whole department was unhappy and the teleworkers definitely had problems. Because we weren't visible we weren't being taken account of in the rearrangements, so there was considerable antagonism between the on-site and off-site workers, each feeling that the other was a threat. I wouldn't say that was a normal or common situation, however. It was because of the reorganization in the company. However, it seemed that it was better to have an off-site manager than to try and work directly for an on-site team, otherwise there were problems with communication.

But what about the impact of teleworking on the rest of Terri's life? For herself she thought the experience has probably increased her self-discipline. Thomas also thought it has made him far more organized and efficient because 'You're always looking for ways in which to save time.' Because your work is lying in the next room waiting to be done, you also have to be firm with yourself about leaving it alone at the end of the day.

Thomas also thinks you have to be disciplined about taking

exercise – something which only vaguely creeps into most people's awareness when they are spending time commuting or rushing around the office or factory floor. As he pointed out, 'It is so easy to come in and just flop and work and eat and work and eat and work and eat and never get out.' The answer? According to Thomas it is: 'Get a big dog – it makes you run all over the place!'

That might not be the solution for everyone, but his point is valid that you do have to find ways of getting the exercise you may very well be lacking in a switch to a more house-bound style of work.

Teleworking and Relationships

In terms of teleworking and relationships Terri said that the only difference there was that her work-based ones had developed over the phone rather than in the office by someone's desk. 'I value my relationships with colleagues and also with clients, and they tend to be quite close and social, although it is obviously mainly on the telephone; but we do have staff get-togethers and there are social events. I feel very aware of that when I'm managing, that some people do get very isolated.'

Thomas echoed her experience. He had wondered whether teleworking would affect his relationships in his working life, but he explained that what actually happened was 'because you're talking to people all the time you actually make a lot more friends. It's like e-mail; you don't see them but you get to know an awful lot of people and you still get their opinion.'

In terms of family relationships, Thomas thinks it is actually a lot healthier for partners to spend the day together. 'I think it's wonderful to be able to spend time together. I think it's unnatural for people either side of the marriage spending half their life with other people. It leads to broken relationships and all that. Four hundred years ago most people actually worked from home anyway. The concept of going off to another building and spending all day in that building with other people probably only started in the 17th century.'

Making the Decision

There are a number of things to consider carefully before making the decision to pursue a teleworking career. It is a very new and very different work option. However, the novelty value could soon wear off, leaving you wondering whether in fact you were suited to it. I asked Terri what she thought you ought to be thinking about before you start out:

> Well, you have to think about all those things to do with motivation, organization, time and space; there are things that will be demanded of you. You have to be the right sort of person to do it. When I was interviewed for my job there was more stress on your personality than there normally would be, and I'm afraid there still is; there are questions which under normal circumstances would be considered rather sexist, about childcare arrangements. When somebody goes into work they assume that childcare has been taken care of, whereas there are some people who think you can work with a toddler playing around in the background. That may work for some jobs, but not with technical authoring. You have to be sure you understand that.
>
> So basically you have to make sure you have the right personality and that teleworking is going to suit you, or else you'll be totally miserable. There's not necessarily a lot of social contact; it obviously doesn't happen in the same way as it would in an office structure. And you have to be sure you're going to get enough of what you enjoy in your workplace. If going down the pub at lunch-time has always been an important part of your day, or if you've always liked having a lot of people around in an office setting, then you're going to miss that. You've got to decide whether the advantages outweigh the disadvantage of losing some of these things.
>
> If you're changing your present job for a teleworking post I would certainly think hard about how your boss is going to manage you, and you do have to think about management

techniques. That doesn't imply bad things, it just means things have to be perhaps a bit more formal. If there isn't already a formal way of passing work from one person to another then this has to be organized.

Terri did not think that balancing the demands of her teleworking career and life was really any different from what most people do in other jobs. Although some may want to telework only while their family is growing up, with the intention of eventually going back into regular employment, Terri feels that teleworking is the only way for her and she wouldn't wish to change.

Thomas was equally enthusiastic and appears totally converted to the teleworking option. He loves the flexibility of being able to get up at 5 o'clock in the morning if he wants and then maybe take a couple of hours in the nice part of the day to take his big dog for a walk – and get his own exercise fix into the bargain.

A Great Equalizer

Thomas pointed out one aspect of teleworking which might easily be overlooked but which will have distinct advantages for some people: 'You don't know that I lost both legs and an arm,' he said. 'Actually I haven't,' he continued, 'but you wouldn't know. I could be blind or anything. There's no way for you to know so it's actually a great equalizer, giving people real opportunity where they haven't had it before. I could be totally disfigured. I could be 76. It equalizes the old and the young, the disabled and the sick. I just think it's absolutely wonderful. As far as the sexes go it equalizes everyone.'

It appears that teleworking has many advantages to offer and may be one of the new work options which appeals to a wide range of people – for a wide range of reasons. Let us take a summary look at the positives and potential pitfalls:

The Pros

Among the pros of teleworking can be counted the following:

- Work can be shaped to fit your own life and its demands, as opposed to having to organize your life to fit in with the demands of your work. It provides you with choice. You can work early in the day, take time off when you want, work late at night, work when the children are at school or when flatmates are out – so long as you get the work done. Your time is more your own.
- You can save time on commuting. Freeing up that one-hour travel time to work can mean an extra ten hours of leisure a week. The stress of commuting also becomes a thing of the past with teleworking, and the savings on travel costs can be considerable – perhaps allowing you to move to a larger house if finding dedicated space at home for teleworking presents a problem.
- Your ability to access or do the work required does not depend on where you live. A real boon for people living in remote rural areas or in employment black-spots.
- You have total control over your work environment, so you can arrange it as it best suits you – perhaps overlooking the garden.
- As a teleworking employee you still have access to company and statutory rights and benefits.
- Teleworking brings with it a greater sense of responsibility which can lead to higher levels of job satisfaction, and most of us respond well to not having the boss watching our every move.
- You will probably find savings can be made on clothes if you normally have to maintain a separate range of outfits for the office.
- Because productivity increases with teleworkers, the stress of mounting workloads may decrease.
- Teleworking removes the barrier to work which physical mobility problems can sometimes create.

- Being embroiled in office politics becomes a thing of the past.

The Cons

Adapting to working as a teleworker raises specific issues which need to be considered beforehand. As you read through the following list of points, others may occur to you, depending on your own circumstances. Make a note of them as you go:

- A dedicated space of some sort is needed. Your employer may advise you of what is necessary and which areas are suitable.
- Keeping your home life, working life and social life separate can be problematic since they all 'occupy' the same space.
- Motivation can be a problem for some. As Terri says, you need to enjoy what you are doing or else motivation can become a big issue.
- Without the real social interaction which normally occurs in your place of work, feelings of isolation can arise. 'Virtual' socializing may not fulfil your own personal needs.
- If your partner or other household members are used to having the exclusive use of the home territory to themselves during the day, your added presence might cause friction and affect the equilibrium of your relationship.
- Promotion may be less easy to come by since your ability to establish or maintain a high profile may be diminished.
- You may feel, or be, excluded from the decision-making processes within the organization.
- Your team-working skills might decline.
- There has been concern in the US about the possible erosion of teleworkers' job security and benefits, as well as an increase in levels of stress.
- The informal way in which you tend to keep up with developments, in both your professional field and the company you work for, disappears.
- Balancing the demands of looking after children and teleworking may be harder than you anticipated.

If you feel that some, or indeed all these issues are of concern to you, read on before you decide that the cons overwhelmingly outweigh the pros. Some issues may be easily resolved with a little forethought, planning or reorganization.

Making It Work

Pre-emptive action can resolve many potential areas of difficulty. Few work situations are ever 100 per cent perfect, so consider what could be done to offset any problems you might envisage in your own situation.

- *If you think isolation might be a problem for you, consider how you could build contact-time into your schedule.* A compromise might be to negotiate spending part of the week back at the regular office or at a telecentre, which will also enable you to keep up your office-based social skills – and keep up with the latest gossip.
- *Establish boundaries with other household members.*
- *Ask your employer, or potential employer, about promotion prospects within the company for people who telework.*
- *Establish how teleworking is organized and managed by the company.* What support structures are in place? What about performance reviews? What targets and objectives are there? What about meetings? How are training sessions organized?
- *Check on both your own and your employer's Health and Safety responsibilities, and establish who is responsible for the maintenance and upkeep of equipment.*
- *You may want to set up an informal mentoring link with one of the office-based workers.* It will help you keep in touch with new developments which might affect you and which you might not hear about until the official memo comes around. (It is also a way of keeping up with the more juicy bits of gossip!)
- *There will be additional expenses for you.* Check with your employer about how these are to be met, including the cost of

making changes to insurance cover. Also check about your tax position in relation to expenses.

- *If your present employers do not have a teleworking system established, approach them with the proposal to convert your existing job, or aspects of it, to enable you to telework.* If they are interested you may want to negotiate a trial period so that you can return to the office if you end up deciding it is not for you. Approximately a quarter of people who try teleworking do not take to it.

Successful teleworking seems to depend a lot on your personality. Your employer may help you assess whether you would be suitable or not. Some of us do need a people-fix more than others, or may have a home situation which really is not appropriate for teleworking. It might help you decide whether teleworking is for you by considering how self-motivated you are and how much you enjoy, or need, to have work colleagues to hand. If you are someone who thrives on the cut and thrust of office politics, and the unofficial pub-based meetings, then full-time teleworking might not be for you. If, on the other hand, you find commuting debilitating or you work better at the crack of dawn when most office doors are still firmly closed, then teleworking could offer you the option you have long been looking for.

CHAPTER FIVE

Job Sharing

We have seen how new ways of working have come about through the need for companies to improve their profitability and competitiveness, and we have seen how some have been spin-offs from developments in new technology. Job sharing is unusual because the stimulus initially seems to have come from the workforce itself, in particular women with commitments to childcare. Now it has been harnessed by many employers, who recognize that it is another tool for helping them recruit and retain women with the skills they want and who would otherwise be excluded from joining the workforce.

What Is Job sharing?

It can be easy to confuse job sharing (which has only been with us since the 1960s, originating mainly in the US) with job splitting, or *twinning* as it is sometimes called (which has been around, certainly in the UK, since the early 1940s), and with work sharing. *Job splitting* is used by employers to create two part-time posts out of what could be done by one full-time person. Jobs which involve more routine work with little responsibility tend to attract job splitting. Depending on which country you live in, splitting a job may benefit the employer but not the employees concerned. *Work sharing* involves dividing the available workload between available staff in order to keep them all gainfully employed and reduce the necessity for laying off people or making them redundant. However, *job sharing* is very different.

Pam Walton of New Ways to Work defines it in her book *Job Sharing: A practical guide* in this way: 'Job sharing is a way of working where two people voluntarily share the responsibilities of one full-time job, dividing the pay, holidays and other benefits between them according to the number of hours worked.'

How a job is shared depends on the requirements of the post and the job sharers' own preferences or other commitments. It can be organized on a split-day or split-week basis, with the sharers working alternate days or alternate weeks, or it can be totally flexible. Arrangements will take into account the tasks involved or the allocation of specific projects or clients. It may be structured to include an overlap period where both job sharers are present at the same time.

More and more job share posts are now advertised, as an increasing number of companies start to offer this option. Ads may be for a new job sharer to join an existing partner or for two people to put in a joint application for a vacancy. It is also not unusual for a full-time post-holder to request that his or her position be converted to job share.

Job sharing puts working part-time into a different framework from normal. It involves team-work with your partner, whereas part-time work usually does not; it enables you to take joint responsibility within the job; it provides you with support as a result of having a work partner; and it removes the sense of isolation which can sometimes accompany part-time working. In general, job sharing widens the scope of part-time work and removes it from its normally lower status in the world of work.

The Present Picture

Job sharing opportunities are mainly taken advantage of by women, although more men are starting to show an interest as they come to appreciate imbalances in their lives, or perhaps want to be more involved in childcare. It also appeals to some people who may have disabilities which preclude them from being able to work full-time hours but who wish to pursue their chosen professional career. Others may be attracted to job sharing as a way of combining other responsibilities or interests. Some have used it to enable them to pursue two careers at the same time, where one of the jobs is not so well-paid, while others have used job sharing to help them establish a foothold in a new profession while changing careers.

In the UK, one in five part-time posts are job shares and a growing 10 per cent of them are now filled by men. It is more widespread in the US, where a recent poll of 155 companies indicated that 74 per cent of them offered job sharing. However, some state laws relating to benefits and hours worked militate against job sharing. Legislation may also be the reason why job sharing is less common in continental Europe, where a more regulated market offers better protection to part-time workers in general.

Job sharing opens up the opportunity for more senior and supervisory personnel to work part-time hours, whereas they might find it difficult to find a part-time post advertised at their particular level. As we will see, the two job sharers I spoke to show that job sharing is far from being a low-status option.

With experience of running job share schemes widening, employers are beginning to realize that although it may involve a slight increase in administrative costs, this is more than offset by the benefits they receive. Productivity is improved, motivation increases, staff turnover drops and they have the assurance of better cover and continuity of service. Not only that, they have the benefit of double the experience and range of skills in one post than they would normally have access to – a case of 'two heads being better than one.' They also gain from being in a position to retain or recruit skilled and experienced staff who might otherwise be difficult to find or keep.

In those countries where job sharing has established a foothold, it is not surprising to find that it is increasing in popularity with employers and employees alike.

The Job share Experience

I spoke to two job sharers about their personal experiences. These two professional women, who found they were able, through job sharing, to pursue their careers, illustrate not only the pluses but also some of the difficulties which may be encountered, and offer some words of advice.

First of all I spoke to Sarah, an architect who job shared for two years in the Housing Department of a local council. She is in her late forties, and is married with three grown children:

Originally I had given up architecture as a job in order to bring up the children. I thought I'd do both jobs badly if I tried to do both at once because architecture is very much a thing with peaks of workloads, so it would be hell raising a family as well. I did some voluntary work while they were growing up and eventually started doing a bit of paid work at the university because that fitted in well with the children, because of the school holidays. That led me on to a research project, also based at the university. It was through that really that I got back into my profession. An architect said to me, 'Why on earth are you doing this cheap contract work when you could be earning properly as an architect?' I thought that because I'd been out of architecture for so long, the chances of my coming back ... well, I hadn't realized quite what the pressure was to recruit people.

So at that point I started looking around for jobs. I simply asked another architect I knew and said 'Surely this isn't right. They wouldn't really employ someone like me?' And he said, 'Well, when can you start?' It was that sort of attitude.

But when I found the job I felt I couldn't cope with full-time; not because of the children anymore but because of all my commitments in the voluntary sector. I said I wanted to do a job share and they said fine, if you can find a partner, which I did at a seminar I attended on women returning to work. We became officially half and half, but in reality I worked far more than the official hours. There was work to be done so I was simply paid *pro rata* for the extra work I did.

I did two years and then there came an opportunity for promotion. I was told I couldn't have promotion in my existing post, but because I was pretty well working full-time by that stage, I thought, 'Well, I may as well get the proper benefits of working full-time.' I was still working for the Housing Committee – it just meant working for a different group leader. I got on to the management rung as the result of the promotion.

When I left the job share my partner continued but without another half. At one stage she increased her hours a bit but I think she has gone back to doing just half because she has younger children. She found it too much.

Job sharing does mean you are part of the staffing in a much more real way than if you're just a part-time worker. Another plus was that it also meant I had more time to do things with the family – and it fit in with my voluntary work.

On the down side, I'm the woman highest up the tree in the division but still I am a woman amongst . . . everyone else is a man, apart from those in administration, and I am still marginalized to some extent – but I can fight. It is this women-against-men thing – that two women are definitely not considered up to what one man is. They think that because you have other commitments elsewhere that you can't get everything done that needs to be done. People expect you to do a full-time job really, even when you are there for only half the time.

It did create additional pressures. The way I endured it was by doing all these extra hours and coping that way.

In the end job sharing proved to be a good stepping stone for me, and I think it's an incredibly important option to have. In the housing association where I do my voluntary work one of the managers wanted to go job share and I think it's terribly important that she is allowed to do that. In some ways an employer does lose out I think because it is a bit more complicated with two people, and to do it properly you really need to provide two spaces because you're bound to have some overlap, but equally, because there are two people who can be flexible, an employer can gain greatly from it.

I suppose it's a bit of swings and roundabouts.

Job sharing changed me in that after having years of really doing somewhat dogsbody sort of jobs I got back into the career structure. When you are a woman at home bringing up children or fulfilling whatever responsibilities you have in the voluntary sector, or doing whatever else you do, you are to some extent second rate in the eyes of the community. But when you are a qualified professional working in a proper job other people's views of you change. I wasn't chair of the housing association before I went back to work as an architect; it was a judge who was the chair. He didn't marginalize me in any way but neither did he treat me as an equal, shall we say? But once I became professional he began to treat me as an equal and he thought 'This woman could do the job and so I can give it up.' Which he did. I'm now chair.

That was a real boost to my self-esteem. It's sad that one is led to do that sort of thing but it does boost your self-esteem, that you can go back and do a professional job. And in turn it affected some of my relationships. My daughter says she's surprised that people are quite impressed when she tells her friends that her mother's an architect. She can't see it herself, and I'm surprised that her friends think it's significant. I suppose I'm a good role model for them.

Also, when I got promoted and started earning a heck of a lot more than I had been, my husband was then able to chuck in work for a year to do a Masters degree to enable him to change professions and that was a great boost to him, the feeling that for a change the income for the family wasn't just his job and he could go and do something he really wanted to do. I think that was significant.

Making It Work

The choice of a partner is terribly, terribly important. The job share with my partner only worked really because we didn't have to share closely at all. We were incredibly different within architecture, with very different outlooks on life. I wouldn't recommend that really. I didn't know the woman beforehand. I just knew she was available, as it were. I think that one can jump into things and be delighted to find somebody who fulfils your practical requirements. It wouldn't have worked really if we had had to work closely.

Also, standing your ground with people who don't think it's going to work is important – because it can work. There was one particular person who simply said 'This can't work because it doesn't fit in with my idea of what I want from people who are working for me. You'll only be here for half the time and it'll be the other half of the time when I think of things I need from you.' The practicalities can seem daunting to the stick in the muds. But no problems like he envisaged arose, and they won't if you're a flexible person, although you have to show yourself to be flexible. This was the other job sharer's problem, that there were certain hours she could be there for and then that was it. That attitude can be because of your personal situation, because of other commitments, but at least a show of willingness to be flexible is important if you want to be accepted.

I also spoke to Kate, who has recently converted her job share of four years as a trades union officer to full-time. By this time her young daughter had begun to attend school and so her daytime childcare responsibilities had begun to decline. It also coincided with a merger of her union and at a time when her job share partner had gone on to be promoted, leaving Kate without a partner.

When I was made redundant from my last job I panicked and thought 'I must get another one.' I had just three months of unemployment and got this job, which was advertised as a job share. It was ideal. It was based out of London, where we were living at the time, and we had wanted to move out, having a young child. So it was an opportunity to move from

66

London and also work half-time, which is what seemed at the time to suit me, so that I could spend half the week on childcare and half on working. I was 38 when I had my daughter. I'd had a career for all those years before, and then she came along and it was really great and I just thought if I worked full-time I was going to miss out really.

So the 35-hour job share post was split down the middle: 17.5 hours contractually, but realistically you're talking of another five hours on top of that. In reality on a full-time basis it would be understood that you'd work more like a 45-hour week rather than 35 hours because of the nature of the work and the travelling, but technically and contractually it was 17.5 hours.

The job share had come about because the woman who had been the full-time officer had gone off on maternity leave, then had come back and made a request that her full-time post be made into a job share. After much difficulty it had been agreed. It was felt it was easier to job share something like a switchboard operator or a clerical or administrative post, but at a more senior level it was very new. She did get it through, and it became the first post at that level in the union that had ever been job shared, nationally. It gave the leeway for other senior staff to consider it, although I should say that there is also a job share agreement in our conditions of employment. What it said was that job sharing would be down to senior management to see whether it was feasible. We divided the week so that my job share partner did the first part of the week and it split at Wednesday lunchtime.

Unfortunately there was no cross-over period. This was something we argued for. It was just done informally, so we met as and when. I used to go round to my job share partner's for a cup of coffee or whatever, or we'd meet at work in our own time. Technically there was no contractual hand-over period. The arguments against it was that we had completely separate areas of work. It wasn't that we had to hand-over but there were things that came up in the other side of the week that we needed to do, so we argued that there should be a hand-over.

I definitely ended up working longer hours because of the job share arrangement, especially with having to find time to talk to my partner. It was never manageable on the 17.5 hours. It was a physical impossibility, apart from the hand-over, because of the nature of the work. We'd get together to go through things under the guise of socializing outside work.

I continued with the job share for four years and then my job share partner became pregnant again. Under the job share agreement if one or other of the partners goes on long-term leave, the other has the first option of covering before it's advertised; so I opted to cover full-time while she was on leave for 15 months. When she returned we converted back to job share.

Eventually my partner applied for a vacant post, which again left me in half a job. Personally I had a fear that if I remained in a job share it would affect my career development in the merger which was taking place; that I wouldn't be given the same status as the full-timers. My partner wanted to progress, so she strategically went full-time for that reason and has subsequently been promoted very high up since then into a senior position.

I stayed as a job share for a year in half a job with the other half not being filled, and in the end I got so fed up with it and also I was working so over my hours that I was concerned that they were going to freeze the other half of the post. So under the agreement I applied to convert the post to full-time. It was granted and it's just as well because there have been redundancies and I think the post would have been frozen anyway because the other unions with which we merged didn't have job share agreements or anyone at officer level job sharing.

Despite the odd difficulties, job sharing enabled me really to value the time I spent at home with my daughter. When she moved on to school last year I then used the time to start a law course, so I found that a real benefit. I could go into work and really look forward to it and really use my time, I felt, quite constructively. Because you know you've only got two-and-a-half days I felt that in some ways I was more organized. Now I can see in comparison, doing full-time, that because I know I've got a whole week I don't always use my time as effectively as I did then. I'm perhaps more likely to spend time chatting (even though I think talking to colleagues is important) than I did when I was job sharing.

The difficulties I did encounter were structural, really. The structure didn't accommodate us. They hadn't worked it out in terms of how the job share would work. There were all sorts of things I thought I should stamp on. For example, when I started, all the staff meetings had been set on Mondays, which wasn't one of my days, so I had to take that up, and a lot of assumptions were made about all sorts of activities, like training. We had computers installed and no account was taken of my working hours. I always had to push it, write memos and say, 'Look I can't be at this meeting.' Professionally I come from a team-working background and really value sharing information with colleagues. I used to get quite fraught about dealing with all this and then feeling like I was whinging. In the end they thought, 'Oh no, she's going on about job sharing again.' I felt as though I was a thorn in the management's side because I had to keep raising it.

Also there was no proper monitoring of the job share by management, which I think is really important because the workload became more and more impossible. By the end of the last year of job sharing I was working a four-day week. I was bringing work home and I just couldn't get out of it and then I suddenly thought 'Who's missing out on this?' and thought 'I am really! I'm better if I do a full-time job.' I was bringing work home and I just couldn't cope with it. Nobody was monitoring it or reviewing it or putting in structure. I put in a load of reports and argued a lot – there was almost another job for me in managing the managers and getting them to supervise it.

My job share partner, I know, felt very differently about it. She'd say that you're only paid for so many hours a week and so why should you do more? But it's easier to see from the outside, and it can be difficult to just say 'No.' But that's the basis of what happened in the end. I just dug my heels in and said 'No.'

I think the job sharing experience did have an effect on me. It changed me. Because the job was a big jump for me professionally (and with it being a job share as well), I was busy running around proving I could do it and absolutely terrified out of my wits, as well as keeping people happy about the job share aspect. The union members I was representing felt unhappy about having what they saw as half a person, so that put a hell of a lot of pressure on. I have to be honest, in the early days it was very unsatisfactory. But I believed in it as a principle, and I still do. But in terms of the employers, if you have an agreement you have to make sure it works, really.

There were very simple things, like I set up a way of recording messages, just a book in the office, and when I left I'd write any messages that might come in for my job share partner. Very simple, but it hadn't been thought of, and it actually took months to come to the conclusion that instead of writing scrappy bits of notes which got lost, or having to ring each other at home, that we should actually create a system whereby we could record important things.

I think flexibility is important in job shares, although at the end I dug my heels in and refused to do anything that didn't fall within the hours because I had got quite angry about the way I felt things were being managed.

I did some training for a local authority which wanted to introduce job sharing. The council officers were very fearful about lots of things, like how you share a job at high level. And yet there are people managing 100 staff who job share quite happily, but for me its success is always down to the fact that the structure has to be right.

If the job had been more clear-cut, what was going to happen was that I was going to work 2½ days a week and my partner at home was going to get a part-time job and work for the other 2½ days, but it became apparent that I just couldn't restrict it like that. So although it was well paid it caused financial difficulties because we were forced to live mainly on just my salary.

What to Look Out For

I would advise people, from the outset, to get various assurances. I think what happened is that we were an experiment so all the problems arose with us. From my experience now I'd talk through the potential pitfalls around the structure, around hand-over times, around managing your work.

I think in a job share the management structure of it needs to be defined. You could be looking at regular meetings, and then maybe every now and again both of you being in the office together. It depends on what the job is, really. Unless it's a completely cut and dried job I'd say work out the structure in advance about communication, about your hours, about hand-over, about how people view you. It's a small point in a way, but I feel quite strongly about people constantly referring to me as part-time. There was a complete lack of understanding that it was a full-time job, with all the rights of a full-time post, but split in half, *pro rata*. Sometimes in meetings I found I had to remind people and explain that part-time is a different ball game.

You must also find out if they have an agreement and go through that. You don't want to make too much of a fuss when you're applying for the job, but once you've got it, it's all right for you to sit down and say, 'Well, how is this implemented?' I'd also find out if the employer/manager has had some training him- or herself.

Sarah and Kate between them provide a good picture of the job share experience and draw attention to some of the many pleasures and pitfalls to be had. Below is a brief summary of some of those pros and cons.

71

The Pros

- It opens up opportunities to work part-time hours, particularly in the professions and senior posts which previously may not have been considered suitable for part-time hours.
- In some countries, job shares offer better conditions of service than are normally available in part-time positions, including better job security and a greater possibility for career progression and promotion.
- People in job shares tend to have a higher standing in other people's eyes than part-timers.
- Job share partners can provide support to each other.
- Job sharing can provide a way in which to find a workable balance to your life.

The Cons

- Finding a suitable job share partner might be difficult.
- It may involve extra hours to establish the job sharing relationship.
- Some line managers, colleagues and support staff might have reservations about accepting the job share situation if it is a new addition to the workplace.

Making It Work

Both job sharers have provided useful pointers to other would-be job sharers. In addition, you may wish to consider the following:

- *Do you find sharing and compromising easy – or do you like to be competitive and perhaps even need to be Top Dog?*
- *Do you enjoy team-working?*
- *Find out if there is a job share agreement within the company and whether the practical management aspects of the job share have been worked out.*

- *Consider how flexible you will be able to be.* At times you may have to accommodate your job share partner's change of plans or the demands of the job itself.
- *If you are interested in this way of working but cannot find a suitable job share vacancy, enquire whether the option is available with advertised posts which do not mention it specifically.* Employers might be willing to consider the option even though they have not included it in the advertisement. Alternatively, find a partner who also wishes to job share and make joint job applications.

If you intend to initiate job sharing with an employer who has had no experience of employing people in this way, it is vital that you work out beforehand the details of how you see it working. And if you intend to make joint job applications you will obviously need to prepare yourselves well for interviews and the many questions the interviewers will want to ask about how you envisage the post working. A chapter in a book like this cannot hope to give you more than a flavour of what it might be like, and hopefully generate interest in this way of working in those people who might benefit from it. So do read up about the finer details about how to work with employers to draw up workable job share agreements (see the Resources chapter, *page 150*).

If you are returning to your profession after a career break you will be in a better position to work out beforehand, possibly with your chosen job share partner, how the job share might work and how you would manage potential areas of difficulty, such as who attends meetings and other issues specific to your work situation. From the experiences of our two job sharers it seems that preparation beforehand can only help to make it a much more fulfilling experience for all concerned, most of all *you*.

CHAPTER SIX

Self-employment

As new work options emerge which satisfy the needs of some employees, others may become disenfranchised with the changes they see taking place around them in the new world of work. Increasingly, some people may begin to feel a sense of uncertainty in their working lives as they witness colleagues, friends or family members fall victim to company rationalization, downsizing and outsourcing programmes. Redundancy and unemployment are spectres that haunt many people; as a result a great many have either chosen or been forced to consider the alternative option to finding work: that of creating it for themselves and becoming self-employed.

Job creation is on the mind and agenda of the governments of most developed nations. As businesses fold amid the rough and tumble of the recession and others take drastic action to retain their competitiveness and profitability, jobs have been lost and many sectors of industry have fallen into decline. Unemployment has risen and appears to be a fixed feature of recent times. This costs a country money – in benefits and in lost revenue from income taxes. It is hardly surprising, then, that self-employment is being encouraged by many of these governments, which see it as one way of helping to reduce unemployment and to create the next generation of jobs and employment opportunities for others. So keen are they to foster growth that many grants, subsidies and support systems are now available. Many people have taken advantage of these opportunities, while others have become self-employed without making use of the help and assistance on offer.

In the UK some 13 per cent of those in work in 1994 were self-employed. This reflects a growth of over 50 per cent since 1979. In Australia almost 10 per cent were self-employed in 1993, while across the European Union there are now well over 21 million people doing their own thing, about one in six (EU figures combine employers with the self-employed). In the US, the home of the entrepreneurial spirit, the figure of 10.5 million self-employed has remained steady over the last five years.

Change can often feel threatening. It wakes us from our comfortable dreams of cruising along towards retirement. But change also brings opportunities. A company which decides to concentrate on its core activities and close down departments in favour of sub-contracting out can be the one which becomes your first client – as you become one of its first self-employed sub-contractors. Redundancy might provide you with the start-up capital for a project you have been toying with for some time. Or a friend's brave step, post-retirement, into this whole new world may inspire you to see the chances cropping up around you.

Change presents us with a chance to re-examine where we are at, and whether we want to stay there. For some, the step into self-employment may take us to where we'd rather be.

Who Does It?

The one great advantage of the self-employed option is that anyone, theoretically, can do it. You do not have to pass the application and selection procedures which might militate against you when trying to find a job. For example, if you have a disability you may have found it difficult to find a post which can accommodate your specific needs – despite Equal Opportunities legislation. Choosing to become self-employed enables you to decide on the sort of business which suits you as an individual. You might want something which fits in with childcare or other caring responsibilities; someone else may want something which can be run from home; others might want the sort of job which enables them to take off every year for three months at a time. Self-employment can fulfil each and every one of these needs. You can design your working life to suit yourself, which is what gives it its appeal and makes it so very different from any other form of employment.

The Opportunities

A lucky few may have an idea for a business which sits nicely on the back burner until the time is right – perhaps when the kids have left home, when the necessary funds have been raised, when an investor is found, when the mortgage is paid off, etc. But for others, a stumbling block can present itself even at this stage: you might not be able to think of something you would do if you were to become self-employed. If this sounds like you, consider the following ways in which to find out what is right for you:

The Skills You Already Have

- work-based skills, above and beyond the main activities of your previous jobs – such as being good with office machines, or at organizing workloads or parties, being good in a crisis, solving people-problems
- leisure-based skills, such as those you have acquired through sports activities, hobbies or around the home and garden
- home-based skills, such as shopping, organizing children's parties, fixing things, devising stories or games

Any of these skills could form the basis of a successful business.

Your Aptitudes

- things you seem to have a 'knack' for, which often amaze other people

- things which you find easy to do, like cheering people up, helping a local group to raise money, making parties go with a real swing

You may find that others are willing to pay for the kinds of things you can do and usually take for granted.

Other people may be more objective and able to help you with this list by reminding you of aptitudes which you might otherwise overlook.

Knowledge You Have Gained

- work-based know-how, such as extensive knowledge of suppliers, how competitors operate, what tools are needed for a particular task
- hobbies you have pursued, perhaps for years
- reading interests which may, over the years, have given you in-depth knowledge of a particular field
- wide-ranging knowledge of a particular geographical area
- knowing 'how to', acquired through years of informal (or formal) research – such as how to raise a perfect dahlia, or pursue a legal claim

You might be surprised to learn that others will happily pay to benefit from the experience you have gained.

Your Experience in Life

- work-based experience, which you could sell in the consultancy field; or think about what your work experiences have taught you. You may often have wondered why someone does not fill a gap in provision which you yourself identified a long time ago.
- life experience often provides the germ of an idea for a business. Over the years you may have gained valuable, and marketable, experience of how to cope with specific family crises, community issues, etc.
- travel may have given you experiences which you could market, for example as a business traveller. Think back on your

travels. You may remember something that happened or that you saw on holiday last year that set you thinking . . .

Your 'Motivators'

- What brings you real enjoyment? What would you do for free, let alone be paid for doing?
- What are you naturally drawn to? What sort of magazines, television programmes, newspaper and magazine articles, books and types of shops?
- What sort of thing gives you a real thrill?

Ask yourself what your dream job would be. It might provide the starting point and give you a sense of direction about where to look for a business opportunity.

If looking within fails to bring ideas, then look further afield and consider the following:

- New experiences can often spark ideas when our daily, known routine fails to inspire, so do something completely new. It need not be anything dramatic. Go somewhere different and find ways in which to meet and talk to new people, who will bring an alternative range of experiences and viewpoints for you to consider.
- Use your senses to spot business opportunities. When you are walking down the street look at cars, shops, shop windows, people, traffic, the weather. Look in the library and browse among shelves you would not normally go near, and read the magazines there which you would never think of buying. Scan through the *Yellow Pages*. Look in bookshops at new publications. Always be looking. Look for inspiration even when you are watching television, and watch out for new trends and new technology which might give you the idea you have been waiting for.

Listen and become an eavesdropper on complaints about the lack of a particular service, quality of service or need for a new product. Listen out for news of local developments, changes in government policy, and talk of new ideas. All of these can open ways for new businesses to develop.

- Talk and let people know you are on the lookout for ideas. Ask them what they do and whether they can see gaps in any markets.
- Consider buying an existing business, or a franchise operation. Find out how they are advertised in your area, or consult the likely trade magazines.
- Survey existing products and services and see how you might improve on them, or go into direct competition, or fill a perceived gap.

Opportunities are often there just waiting to be acted on by someone who is quick and alert enough to recognize them. Once you start to look around you might be surprised at how soon a list of ideas can be generated. It is as though you have re-tuned your antennae – suddenly all manner of suggestions and possibilities present themselves.

A Story of Success

One man who appears to have had his antennae set correctly and who has come to the attention of the British public is Daniel Wagner. In an article in the *Sunday Telegraph* (20th March, 1994), he discussed his path to success. He had no particular training when he set up his business; indeed, neither did he have any money since he was unemployed and living off state benefits. He left school when he was 17, but by the time he was 30 his company was being floated on the UK Stock Exchange for almost £90 million.

He spotted his business idea at the age of 21 while working for an ad agency. He had been asked to find out about the data communications market, realized as a result that there was little in the form of good research databases, and so on spotting the possibilities he promptly handed in his notice and began working on setting up his own business, Market Analysis Information Database (MAID).

With only savings from his benefit cheques he invited a potential business client to lunch – and won him over. Thus he took his first step towards becoming a millionaire. It was not without its difficulties, though, as business rarely is. Although he had won over that vital first client, he then only managed to sign up another two in the first year of trading. On instinct he went to New York, set up three appointments and successfully managed to win all of them over. He was set to make his mark and things obviously went from strength to financial strength from then on.

It only takes that initial spark of an idea to set you off. No megabucks are a pre-requisite, or MBAs, or 'good' connections. The door is open to anyone in the new world of self-employment.

The Self-employed Experience

Like much in life, there are no guarantees about being self-employed. Your venture may not succeed as well as Wagner's has done – or indeed, succeed at all. Let's face facts, the majority (90 per cent) of new businesses fold within the first five years. You would think this would be enough to send each entrepreneur scurrying back to join the millions sending off new job applications each week. But not so. Although the failure rate of businesses is high, some 80 per cent of those who do become self-employed, stay self-employed. The experience appears to be worth it.

I spoke to Donald, a television producer, about what he thought of being self-employed after years as a staff reporter on a national daily newspaper in the UK. He said he has thoroughly enjoyed it, especially being able to invent your own market. Like many people, he thinks being self-employed gives you great freedom. 'There's no other way to live, really. You can become whatever you want to become.'

However, Donald did sound a few words of caution:

80

Unfortunately, I think everyone believes they can do it – and not everyone necessarily has the skills to do it successfully.

Also, you can't turn down work and it's difficult to go on holidays. There's no security, and you've got to earn a lot of money to make any provision for your future. You're also subject to fashion very much. There is often a long delay between doing work and getting paid for it. Holding back on payment is an increasing problem with consumers of your service or product.

But despite it all it's better than sitting on your butt and hoping something will come your way, because it won't. You've got to get out there and go and do it.

I would add that I think it's important if you're married that both partners support each other. It can be very hard on a marriage because of the uncertainties. It can put a strain on relationships. I also think it's important not to be frightened and to believe in yourself.

From my own experience, too, I agree that being self-employed does give you a wonderful sense of freedom, one which I do not think can compare with other sorts of employment. Yes, it is equally true that one is less secure, in terms of there being no guarantee of money in the bank at the end of the month. But being self-employed can give you such a thrill, knowing that you are managing to survive by the work you do; that through your very acts you benefit and generate the money to pay your bills. There is an exquisite pleasure in finding another client, selling another idea, and having that freedom to choose what you do when you want to. If a bit of filing is all that you can manage on one day, so be it. The next may find you steaming ahead into the small hours. You have the option of being able to work with your own energy flow, so you are always getting the best out of yourself.

Studs Terkel in his book *Working* reflects on his own experience of being self-employed in radio, too. 'I'm able to set my own pace, my own standards, and determine for myself the substance of each program. Some days are more sunny than others, some hours less astonishing than I'd hoped for; my occasional sloven-liness infuriates me . . . but it is, for better or worse, in my hands . . . Though my weekends go by soon enough, I look toward Monday without a sigh.'

He manages to put his finger on important points in that short paragraph, because the reality is that there are ups and downs in self-employment with which to contend. Even though it is immensely enjoyable, it is certainly no easy ride. And what can make it less comfortable is finding out that you, and you alone, have to bear the responsibility of deficiencies in your ways of working. It affects you and your business now, whereas before it may merely have irritated someone else – your boss perhaps. And as Terkel's words imply, self-employment is much like being married; you do have to stick by yourself, for better or worse. Having staying power and commitment is important if you are to be successful at working for yourself. But in exchange for taking on such awesome responsibilities you are also given the power and freedom to make of it what you will.

The Pros

- Independence
- A greater degree of control over your life
- The opportunity to manage the risks yourself
- The chance to organize your work to fit in with your other life aims
- Despite the risks involved, self-employment may ultimately be more secure than being employed, where redundancy can strike anyone at any time and without much notice. If things are not going too well with your own venture, at least you know from day to day what the state of affairs is.
- A great sense of achievement
- The chance to play to your strengths and do what interests you

The Cons

- Money. Until the business becomes established your earnings might be below what you would otherwise have earned in employment.
- Hours. You will probably work longer hours, especially in the early days.
- The failure rate is high for new businesses.
- Stress levels can be high.
- It can be bloody hard work!

(See also Chapter 4, which looks at some of the particular difficulties of working from home.)

Making It Work

Many books have been written about how to set up a business and go about working for yourself, but here are some brief points to consider before you sink all your savings and energy into your venture of a lifetime:

- *Research, research, research.* It is vitally important to do the groundwork and preparation beforehand and resist the temptation to get the business cards printed and start trading from next Monday morning before you have really checked things out. How depressing and foolhardy it would be to start trading as a computer engineer, only to realize there isn't a PC within a hundred miles of where you live, or to open a nursery when there are only retired couples in your catchment area. Research your product/service; your market (do people really want to buy – you can only find out by asking them); locations; skills needed; finance.
- *Use the information you have gleaned from all your research to draw up a business plan.* This is not just an academic exercise, but a document which will help you to sell your idea to

potential backers. You will also need it yourself to use as a guide for your business; to see whether things are going according to plan and, if not, to take the necessary action to put things right. A business plan covers: a description of the proposed business; your unique selling point (what makes you different from the rest); funding plans; cashflow projections; pricing; the competition; results of market research; marketing – how markets are going to be accessed; premises; location; capital expenditure requirements; staffing; anticipated growth and development of the business, and any other points relevant to your specific business idea.

- *Make sure you have secured adequate finance beforehand.* Under-funding is one of the main reasons that businesses go under.
- *Do a 'skills inventory' on yourself and find out what your limitations are.* Remedy those you can through training courses, or arrange to buy in missing skills from others.
- *Consider whether you have the necessary qualities for being self-employed.* Commitment, motivation, being able to take risks and handle responsibilities are just some of the things you need to be happily and successfully self-employed.
- *Consider sharing the burdens of running a business by being self-employed in partnership with other like-minded souls.*
- *Find out what government support is available.* Finance, advice, business training, export advice and business support may all be available in one form or another where you live, especially if you are in an area which has been badly hit by unemployment.
- *Ask for help.*
- *Go to your local library for books on how to set up your own business.*

These changing times have brought many casualties, but equally they have thrown up their share of opportunities. Self-employment is one such opportunity as downsizing and outsourcing open up new markets for people to become providers of services. You might decide to step into that breach and perhaps take advantage of some ready-created markets which you may have intimate knowledge of through your previous employment. But while self-employment can be incredibly rewarding, it is not for the faint-hearted, nor the foolhardy. If you think it may be what you have been looking for, do your homework and preparation, expect to do some hard work – and reap the sorts of rewards you could otherwise only dream of.

CHAPTER SEVEN

The Co-operative Option

In the last chapter we looked at the option of self-employment, which offers a great deal more freedom – and possibly more security – than a traditional nine-to-five job. But it can take a great deal of courage to leave what people still feel is the security of having an employer, and launch out on your own. The responsibilities are heavy and may be more than some people want to take on board. If only there were another way. Well, you will be pleased to hear there is. Co-operatives offer that very opportunity – to escape from regular employment and be involved in the setting up of a new business without having to shoulder all the responsibilities yourself.

What Is A Co-op?

There are many different elaborations on the definition of what a co-op is, but broadly speaking a co-op is a business which belongs to the people who work in it – all of them. Everyone who chooses to become a member of the co-operative in which they work has a vote and an equal say in how the business is run, organized and developed, thus sharing in the overall responsibilities. There is no one owner. Everyone is of equal status, even though some may fulfil management functions and others be involved in shop floor or clerical work.

Unlike regular companies, any profits generated through the co-op's activities are for the benefit of its member employees, not just to line the pockets of the employer or anonymous outside shareholders, as is normally the case. However, having said that, some co-ops may choose to be open to non-employee members as well.

Co-ops can be broadly grouped into the following types:

Agricultural/fisheries co-ops: these enable lone farmers and fishermen to benefit from acting collectively to market produce and buy expensive equipment.

Consumer co-ops: set up to enable food to be bought in bulk for its members, who are also its customers. Cost savings are passed on to members.

Service co-ops: these are the same as consumer co-ops, except that a service, not produce, is provided for its members.

Housing co-ops: where a property is owned and controlled by the people who live there together.

Workers' co-ops: commercial businesses which are, at least in the UK, the most common sort of co-op.

Their Development

The phenomenon of people working co-operatively has been taking place world-wide for many centuries. Acting together is seen as a way of achieving more than would otherwise be possible.

The International Co-operative Alliance represents co-operatives world-wide, including those in North America, South America, Africa, the Middle East and Asia. In both developed and developing nations co-operatives can be found to be flourishing, whether in rural or urban settings.

We have seen in previous chapters how the recession has brought with it new opportunities for businesses, as many companies make strategic decisions to concentrate on core activities and use sub-contractors. Mass unemployment has created a pool of talented people looking for ways in which to secure a working future for themselves. These circumstances have come together and sparked an interest within groups of like-minded people to try and remedy their situation by working together. Forming a co-operative has offered the way forward for many such people.

Co-ops enable individuals to become active members of the workforce. It offers the opportunity to devise a way of working which suits the flexibility needed by its members. It also enables doors of opportunity to be pushed open into areas which might otherwise be all but locked to them. For example, one group of women who were employed, unhappily, as cleaners decided to band together, form their own co-op, and have now become successful businesswomen. Without taking advantage of being able to set themselves up as a co-operative, they might not otherwise have gained the independence and experience they have.

At present there are over a thousand worker co-ops in the UK alone, employing almost 9,000 people in businesses as diverse as building, graphic design and computing. They have been set up as a result of employee buy-outs of existing companies faced with closure (sometimes referred to as 'phoenix co-ops'); as conversions of successful businesses by management and employees; or as new starts – the most common. Across the EU there are around 45,000 co-ops with a total membership of approximately 750,000. More than 50 per cent of these co-ops are in Italy, where state funds are available to support co-operative developments. Australia boasts over 2,000 co-ops which between them have an estimated asset base of $3.7 billion and which managed a turnover estimated at $5.4 billion in 1992/93.

In the US, Employee Share Ownership Plans (ESOPs) are popular, although these are different from true co-ops in that the apportionment of power is related to how many shares you hold. This has not detracted from their appeal, however, since there are now approximately 11 million people in ESOPs in the US.

What Does It Entail?

Initially, all it needs is a group of like-minded individuals to come together with the same resolve, that of creating work for themselves which benefits them all directly and in which they all have an equal say. You may be disenfranchised in your present employment, or want to find a way to improve your situation (as the cleaners did), or you may simply want to forge a way back into employment.

Many opportunities exist. Just think about how often local people, neighbours, friends or work colleagues have identified and talked at length about some common area of difficulty, dissatisfactions, gaps in provision, a gap in the market for a new product, a new market which current bosses are reluctant to enter, of how things could be, of disagreements with the ideals of employers, and so on. Each of these situations could represent the starting point for collective and co-operative action.

I spoke to two people who have taken the step and joined with others to form their own successful co-operatives, both of which are very much thriving businesses despite the recession, which has seen many other 'mainstream' operations go under. They told me about their experiences of working in a co-operative, which can hopefully give you some idea of what it might entail and what you might expect.

The Co-operative Experience

Iain is 33 and single and is one of the founder members of a successful graphics company in Scotland. He talked to me about his own personal experience of what it has been like for him to set up and work in a worker's co-op.

It started in 1989 when three of us, the three founder members, were working together in a community print room on a government-sponsored community programme. We didn't know each other before then. We were there on a one-year scheme and we quite enjoyed it. It gave us a really

89

good grounding, although it was very much at the lower end of what we do now. So, we just decided that we quite liked that line of work and that we liked working together and that the only really down side of what we were doing was the structure that we worked in. The whole place was run by a director who wasn't a brilliant manager of people. He tended to rub people up the wrong way, and we just thought that if we could do something like this and just work collectively that it would be brilliant.

When the year on the programme came to an end we all drifted off with the intention of getting together a few months later and getting working on it. We took a few months off; Anne went travelling round the world; me and Cheri just hung around and took it easy. Then we started meeting up, and over about a year we got everything organized and set up.

Myself and Anne had both had previous experience of co-ops and knew what it involved. It was obviously an attractive way of working. Being a co-op means that we're directors; we control the company in every way. If we were in partnership and we owned the company, the biggest problem would have been that if someone had decided that he or she wanted to leave, we would have had to buy them out. They would have been entitled to a third of the company's assets, which would have just broken it completely. It was the safety thing as well. We deliberately set it up so that we only had £1 shares so that the co-op would survive any one of us leaving, and if we wanted new people we didn't want them to have to buy their way in. We wanted other people to be able to join us easily, so we decided on the £1 share.

Just gone two years ago we had a fourth member join us. We got to the point where we had too much work, so we advertised. We had 200 people apply. We hadn't taken anyone on before and we didn't really know what we were doing. We interviewed far too many people: 20. It took weeks and weeks – we learned a lesson from that. At the end of the process Ron came out of it, and it's been fantastic. He ended up being exactly the right person and was prepared to give the kind of long-term commitment we wanted.

Now we all do some design work. Ron and Cheri are full-time designers, but it involves liaising with customers, doing some of their own reprographics, their own quotations and their own invoicing. Anne does more admin; about 50–50 admin and design. She gets the scheduling side of it and managing the print work. I do as little design as possible. I tend to look after the technical side of things, particularly the computers, and the book-keeping and the payroll. We're looking for another designer because we're a bit top-heavy with admin at the moment and if we had another designer we could take on more work and it would be better for all of us. We all work full-time.

Almost all our work comes from voluntary organizations. We do some work for local authorities but we've only one commercial client and they're always top of the list when it comes to difficulties getting money out of people. We're very wary of commercial clients. We're careful about whom we work for, morally and politically as well as for financial reasons, but we're not overtly political at all.

What You Get Out of It

I asked Iain what he got out of working in a co-op.

I'm just happy with it. I find it so fulfilling; the motivation has stayed. I've never not wanted to come to work in the morning. I zip into work full of beans and I just enjoy it.

I suppose it's because we like working together; we enjoy each other's company. We're always talking about stuff and listening to music all day (while we work). We work very hard but it's very relaxed here, i.e. informal. You don't have any boss breathing down your neck.

We all get on very well; we socialize a fair bit together, so that makes work quite fun and I enjoy the actual nitty-gritty bits of my job – the technical bits, and I actually love book-keeping. I discovered a couple of years ago that I enjoyed it more and more and more, so I'm pushing my job in that direction. I try to get away from doing design work. I find design is the side I like least because there are always deadlines and I'm the sort of person who, as a deadline approaches, gets more and more stressed; and I'm terrible for putting things off until the last minute, and so I always have horrible stress when it comes to design work.

Essentially we all try to do what we're good at, and also what we enjoy – they tend to be the same thing. We've got quite a diverse range of skills here so luckily we can all do mostly what we enjoy doing.

I think part of why we get on well together is because we are a co-op. No one's really marginalized, we can all have an input and so we all feel motivated. We feel it belongs to us, even though we've only got our £1 share, but it does in every other sense belong to us. We're controlling our own destiny; planning ahead, like this year we've all started thinking about buying flats. We've just got to the point where we can afford that. I think we've just realized how long term the whole thing is. We've got jobs for as long as we want them. It's very stable; we're gradually increasing our standard of living and we're planning ahead a bit more.

I also find that having no boss is a huge benefit. It's been such a long time now since any of us have had one that I think we'd find it unbearable if we had to go back to a nine-to-five with someone telling you what to do. I don't think any of us could stand it. There's the feeling of having control of what's going on: our work environment, everything we do. We've more or less made it up as we've gone along: our work practices, our internal rules, the way we do just about everything we've learned on the job and made it up. We just really like that. We've got complete control of it.

It may sound very dynamic but it doesn't move forward as quickly as we would like. We have plans and visions about what we would like to do and then we get bogged down in what we have to do. Days just fly by and then we find we haven't done things we planned to do, and we're going much more slowly – but we're getting there.

I suppose we tend to be less organized than we would like to be. Having said that, looking at a lot of the ordinary businesses, a lot of the people we come across seem a lot less organized than we are, although some are better. We tend to get bogged down in the work and no one says, 'Hey it's about time we had a meeting because this needs sorting out.' Because we're all bogged down in our work we're all just happy to leave it and get on with what we're doing. If it was someone's responsibility to say, 'Hey it's about time we had that meeting because we've things to sort out,' then it would happen a lot more often. Instead we just sit around the table, look through the work that's going on and then talk about anything longer term. It's all completely unstructured.

Looking back I'm sure the hours we worked have been a lot longer than we'd like. I'm also sure that if, five years ago, we'd all just gone off and got jobs we would have earned a lot more money and worked a lot less hours; but now we're getting to the point where the hours are shrinking and the money's increasing and we're reaping the benefits. So I don't really begrudge all the unpaid overtime we had to put in in the early days. We've got something to show for it now.

I feel very confident about the future. I suppose working in this co-op, for the first time I can see the rest of my life stretching out; can see I'm quite happy in doing what I'm doing and that I'll be very happy doing it for a long time. Nothing I've done before has given me that feeling; a sense of fulfilment. I feel happy and contented. I'm happy thinking I'll probably be here in five years' time, whereas when it first started we thought, 'How long do you think we'll stick with this?' Up until then I'd been quite a restless person; I couldn't see me sticking with anything for more than two/three/four years, but now we're in year six.

Over the years, working in the co-op has affected some of my relationships, in so far that I tend to be wrapped up in work and have not as much time outside our immediate scene here as I would like. That's been improving over the last year or two; the hours have dropped and we don't have to do as much overtime and we're getting the weekends off – we used to have to work most weekends at busy times, and that doesn't really happen any more – so that's improving.

My family are really happy with what I'm doing. I think their view is that I'd messed around for so long and done all sorts of things in my twenties, so my parents are quite content at seeing me self-employed. So there's been good and bad. Just the sheer amount of time I've had to devote to it over the years; it takes up the space in your head, if you know what I mean. It's hard to stop thinking about it. When you've worked late your head's still full of ideas and you go home and you don't really want to talk about anything else. Anne and I have been partners for the past three years and that works out really well because we don't have to stop talking about it if we don't want to. We can just wander off together and natter on about the future things that are coming up and possible developments.

Sometimes when partners work together it can lead to problems and at first I was wary because the co-op I worked in before was founded by a couple and that turned out to be a disaster. Everyone felt that their relationship was unfair on everyone. I think while Anne and I are at work we just tend to get on with the job and not really relate as a couple – we leave that for outside of work. In fact we don't see enough of each other. We're at the office all day long, tied up with work, and we feel we don't get enough time together outside of it.

All in all I think part of our success is because of the planning we did. We spent a whole year beforehand working on a business plan. I think I'd say planning is essential, and compatibility between people. Perhaps we've been lucky; we're quite relaxed with each other and take up as little psychological space as possible. We had someone join us temporarily, but somehow he just couldn't fit in. It wasn't ego, it was something else. He just couldn't blend in. So personalities are important if you're thinking of joining or setting up as a co-op.

I think the best advice I could give anyone is just to go for it. It's really worth while when it works and I can't think of anything else to beat it. And I'd like to say to those who aren't thinking about setting up a co-op, to think about it. I think more should consider it as an option. When it works it's brilliant. When it doesn't, it's not any worse than any other way of working.

If you're interested you do need to find out more. We had access to a local Co-operative Development Agency, and the amount of detail they made us go into was really useful, and the things that came up were things we'd never have thought of. So get in contact with your local development agency because there may be subsidies available. They gave us a grant of £1,000 for market research and to do our business plan and in the end they gave us a loan of £5,000.

I then spoke to Johan, an ex-teacher in his mid-forties who is married with one child. Like Iain, he was one of the founders of the co-op in which he works, which markets recycled paper. The co-op started in the early 1980s with just two people. Over the years it has grown in size and there are now 28 people involved with the company. Apart from the main base, another two sales offices have opened in other parts of the country, and turnover is in the millions.

Concerned at the number of hours Iain said he had put in, I started by asking Johan how many he worked:

Well, it's less now than it used to be. When it first started it wasn't too bad; it was still fairly small. It was probably around 50 hours a week. But come the later years it went up to 60/70 hours a week which was ridiculous really but that's the way we thought we ought to get the business running. Now it's slightly down again to 45/50 hours a week. This applies to me. It doesn't apply to everyone here; some others perhaps, but not everybody.

Johan then went on to talk about what working in a co-op has meant to him:

> Working in a co-op gives you challenges as well as opportunities. The positive side of it is the informal nature of the business and the involvement I suppose of everyone here, in theory to some extent, in important decision-making. It's certainly very important to me that there has been the opportunity for everyone who works here to become a member, and if you're a member you've got a vote in important decisions which may affect the future of the business.
>
> Personally it's something I feel is very close to my personal preferences as a form of organization. I'm reluctant to work for a very large multi-national organization because as individuals you tend to get lost in the system and you're a number rather than an individual. That's important to me and I'm sure it's important to most of the people here.
>
> To the outside world I think co-operatives are still considered as alternative, rather suspicious, perhaps financially unsound. That unfortunately is the view held by a lot of people in the financial world. Co-ops are not fully accepted, I think, as commercial enterprises in their own right, although that has changed a little bit over the years; but that is still the view held by financial institutions. It's difficult to find sources of financial backing if you're a co-operative.
>
> In terms of working in a co-op the organizational structure and decision-making process can be slightly longer (although not always) than it might be in a conventional company where one person just dictates the speed of decisions rather than consult and communicate. Consultation and communication are fairly high up on the agenda here.
>
> Making sure people who work in the co-op are aware of co-operative principles is a challenge. To have them join as a member and take on the full responsibilities that go with ownership of the business is more of a challenge now than it was in the early days, a) because we are bigger and b) because of the financial commitments that go with ownership, are

much larger now, so it is a slightly bigger step for people to take.

Over the last three years we've consolidated what we did in the early years. Like any growing company, or growing co-op in this case, one goes through a watershed, organizationally. Initially there were two of us involved doing everything from book-keeping to delivery to telesales; of course as you develop as a company the jobs become more specific and we now recruit people specific to a particular job, whether it's telesales or warehousing or delivery or book-keeping or purchasing, so that's something which will develop further.

Also, in terms of the organizational structure we initially had two people who were members of staff and who were also directors, whereas now the situation is a bit more complex, because now we have a board of directors with executive power which is elected by the members on an annual basis. There is also a management structure in place now, with a general manager and departmental managers. The departmental managers are answerable to the general manager, and the general manager is answerable to the board of directors, and the board of directors is in turn answerable to the membership. The membership is at the top of the pyramid; a reverse pyramid.

A co-op offers flexibility in terms of career development, which may be more difficult to find in a conventional company. In a co-op you feel that you have something to offer and that you can develop in other jobs and shift sideways or up or down or whichever way you want to go in terms of career development. You have more opportunities. Here, if someone has particular talents and is prepared to give it a go then we obviously will do so. It is important to know what type of co-op it is and how it operates, depending on the challenges you want to take on. I think it's important to find out a little more about the background of co-ops perhaps before you join.

If you're interested in setting up a co-op, the three key words are: self-motivation, determination and stamina.

Basically you determine the fate of the business yourself, rather than in a nine-to-five job where you sit back and don't think about the consequences of what you do. Your input can be seen in a very effective way and most co-ops, if they are successful, operate some form of profit-related pay or benefit scheme which directly benefits the employees. So if you are successful it is a very direct way of seeing the fruits of your labour.

The Pros

Iain and Johan have described the benefits which they personally have experienced from working in a co-op. Many of the others you might expect are those which relate to being self-employed and master of your own fate. The added bonus is that the overall risk and responsibility is shared out and not shouldered by just one person.

Because the business is controlled by each and every member equally, there is no boss telling you what to do and no longer the likelihood that unpleasant and unwelcome decisions will be sprung on you by callous managers and employers. Sudden closure is less of a threat since a co-operative can continue trading so long as it is managing to stay afloat. In dire times, members of a co-op might vote to take a slight cut in wages or make other changes to ensure the co-op's continuing success. Since each employee-member has a vested interest in the business, choosing to make sacrifices where necessary is an option which many happily take. Having that amount of control over their working lives and futures is one of the most important benefits for many who work in co-operatives.

The Cons

Despite its appeal, some may see not being able to make sole executive decisions as a distinct disadvantage. Let's face it, some people are power junkies and the thought of sharing the decision-making process and the profits with others would be anathema to them.

The difficulty in raising finance has been mentioned, as has the input which may be required from members in the initial stages. This is often difficult for any new enterprise, but it seems more so perhaps for co-operatives.

Making It Work

Although anyone can set up a co-op since you do not need any special qualifications, as Johan pointed out you do need commitment, self-motivation, and be prepared to put in a lot of effort. Think about whether each potential co-op member has these qualities beforehand.

- *Contact your local co-operative agency to find out how they can help you.* Your local library should be able to point you in the right direction if you are not sure where to start.
- *Arrange for an existing co-operative member to talk to those who have shown an interest in setting one up.*
- *Make sure you have the same aims in wanting to set up a co-operative.* If you are not pulling in the same direction, unnecessary friction could result.
- *You want your enterprise to succeed, so establish what business skills are needed and what existing skills people can contribute.*

Co-operatives are no 'easy option'. At the end of the day they are still businesses which need to operate as a going concern, and which need commitment from members to do so successfully. But although it is not an easy option, it does make the route to running your own business possible and much easier than might otherwise be the case if you tried to go it alone.

As Iain urged, more people who have not thought before about setting up a co-op, should. Perhaps that might include you.

CHAPTER EIGHT

Community Businesses

The previous chapter showed how groups of individuals can join together in a co-operative as a way in which to create their own employment and reap the benefits themselves. Another option which offers opportunities for creating your own employment is to work with others to create a community business. Although similar to co-ops, they are not quite the same, as we shall see.

Definition

Imagine the scenario: a group of unemployed tradespeople with years of experience and a whole range of skills between them. Imagine then the excitement when the news breaks that a large commercial development is going to be built in the local area. Then imagine the disappointment as each visit to the local Job Centre shows no new jobs being advertised and that, instead, the work is being handled by contractors using labour from out of town. The building work which should be bringing many jobs to an area desperate for them is instead going to others.

This is what happened to Rob, who had a good moan about it over a cup of tea with one or two others he met at a residents' association meeting. Not surprisingly, they felt the same way. Perhaps most people would have left it at that; feeling better for having had their grievances aired, but then going away still angry and bitter about the situation they found themselves in. Instead, this group of men decided to take control of the situation and do something about it together. They wanted work, and agreed that if they could not get any on their own, perhaps they could if they worked at it together and combined their skills and expertise. So was born their community business in building work.

Community businesses are different from ordinary commercial operations, which make profits only for their owners. They are also different from co-ops, which may have a more social focus but which also distribute profits only among co-op members. Although community businesses are commercially-run enterprises, their profits are ploughed back into the community – either to create more jobs, fund new community businesses, or to pay for non-income-generating projects – and generally help to create a ripple effect in social and economic regeneration; profits are not distributed to individuals. So if your aim in life is to become a millionaire, this is not the way to go about it! If, however, you want to make a difference to the area you live in and create employment for yourself and others into the bargain, then setting up a community business could be the way forward.

Since community businesses are enterprises which aim to benefit an area economically and/or socially, seed capital and grants are often available from local councils, government agencies or other interested parties. It is not up to individuals to find the money for start-up costs out of their own pockets. However, although community businesses may have strong links with such bodies, they are run with the aim of becoming financially independent and must therefore be run along commercial lines – and must make money.

Community businesses are essentially owned by the community which they serve. Their focus is on creating the employment which seems to be denied them through other more traditional routes. They help to bring economic regeneration back to an area; they can have as few as two people involved, or may be huge enterprises with an annual turnover of millions of pounds. The important element is that community businesses are owned and controlled by the local community. Every person involved has a vote in how it is run, deciding everything from what everyone should be paid to how the business should be marketed.

Community businesses may choose to operate as a limited company; a community co-op; or as an umbrella organization for other trading initiatives (as we shall see with Bill's set-up).

Community businesses are not voluntary organizations or ways just to occupy your time which would otherwise be idled away. They are not for do-gooding or for novel ways in which to socialize. They are set up as professional operations with commercial aims. The only way in which they differ from more traditional companies is that their success is shared to benefit the whole community. They provide help for a neighbourhood or locality, in ways that are best for it.

How They Come About

As with Rob and his friends, a community business can come about as the result of unemployment and the refusal to accept the status quo. They are born out of people's desire to reclaim control over their lives and where they live, to gain a sense of independence and identity. Many want to use community businesses to wrest control from authorities, professionals and employers who may not be working in the best interest of a community. They provide the opportunity of work which they can organize in such a way as to accommodate the needs (for example, for flexibility) of particular groups of people who would otherwise be prevented from entering the job market. The strong desire to do something about regenerating an area and making it economically active again is the driving force behind most successful community businesses.

Examples of Community Businesses

Almost any activity can form the basis for a community business, so long as it reflects the needs of the community in which it is based. Here are some examples:

- a retail shop
- nurseries
- cafés
- contract cleaning
- publishing and printing
- painting and decorating
- security business
- business centres
- catering
- energy conservation
- manufacturing
- and so on.

But let us take a look at what Rob and Bill have to say about what it is like to work in a community business. Their operations are very different. The one Rob is involved in is small and very much in its infancy, whereas the one Bill works for is much larger and is further down the road in its development.

The Community Business Experience

Rob is an electrician living in London. As he said, 'It's bad enough being unemployed, but to look at work going on in your area being done by out-of-town contractors is like rubbing your nose in it.' And so, together with some like-minded others, he decided to do something about it. They set up their own community business offering building services to local residents and businesses, including their own local council.

There were six of us initially but three have gone on and found jobs. There are three of us now; a decorator and two

103

of us electricians. We've also paid for someone's registration with the gas trades association so that he'll be able to start work with us too. He couldn't afford that himself with him being unemployed. Whenever we need new people I advertise the posts through the local Job Centre.

We're all classed as employed because we set up the business as our own limited company. The council helped us with all that so that we could go on their list of approved contractors. We also received advice and help to do a cashflow projection sheet and prepare a marketing plan, and then we applied for grants from organizations using a directory of grant making trusts. We got £2,000 towards a van from one of them.

You do need some sort of financial injection at the beginning. We had £500 from the first job we did. They were quick in paying us so we had a working cashflow straight away, more or less. Then we had a £9,000 job so that helped us, and between the two of them it gave us a kick start, but now it has come to the stage where we are £2,000 overdrawn but we are owed nearly £6,000.

I must admit I've had a year of it and sometimes I've said I've had enough and I'd rather just work for someone, 8 a.m. to 5 p.m.; forget about work and chasing money owed. I know I'd have had more work if I'd been working for someone. If I didn't have the money worry it'd be all right because there's lots of ways of getting work and there's loads of work out there but it's the cashflow which is a problem. Still, we turned over £27,000 in our first year.

Being based in a community centre has helped and has given us credibility. We did a leaflet drop around the area and a woman phoned us up as a result and said that because we were in the community centre we weren't a fly-by-night company which was going to make a load of money and be gone the next day. She knew she could ring up the community centre and say 'Where's that organization?' Because we're based in the community centre you also meet lots of people who need things doing for them, like elderly people;

that's where we get a buzz. There's no money involved but it's where you get satisfaction. That's the good thing, all the spin-offs.

Obviously one of the other good things to come out of setting up this community business is employment. We've managed to create our own jobs.

I enjoy doing it and, like I said, trying to help someone if they can be helped by giving people work is great. We take on people with learning difficulties when we can, because they can find it hard to get work normally.

There have been other spin-offs, too. I've made a lot of friends and contacts. I've also acquired a lot more skills. Setting this up enabled me to get work with another voluntary organization which gave me more experience in that field too.

Besides the cash problems, I can't think of any disadvantages to setting up a community business. Cashflow is always a problem, but that's true with every business whether you're private or community. Doing the work, finding it, making the tea and doing the accounts we've found is a bit too much to do all at once. You really need someone to co-ordinate or run it.

I like to think that working in the community like this has perhaps made me a nicer person because it's had a personal impact on me doing jobs for, like, elderly people. We must be doing something right because people seem to want to keep in touch with us once we've done work for them.

My plans are to see this running itself and perhaps go and start another one somewhere else where there is high unemployment – but with the right help. I wouldn't do it the same way I've done this.

All you need is to get five people, no matter where it is. Get a group of tradesmen together, keep it ticking over for a year, get the accounts set up, and approach your local council for help. There's a lot of publicity available for things like that. We had plenty of publicity. But you need financial help even just to keep the wages going, at least for the person who's managing it. You need proper funding.

If you want to start one yourself I'd suggest that you get in touch with your local residents' association because they've always got premises like this. Get some leaflets printed. Keep your overheads to a minimum. Don't open any accounts with suppliers unless you have to, so that you don't owe anyone any money. Pay as you go along.

You can also use your experience in the community business to go and get another job. It all helps on the CV. You could use it as a springboard. It really does open up opportunities.

Rob's venture is in its infancy and is quite a small concern at present, although he knows there is great potential, based on his intimate knowledge of the area.

In contrast, Bill is involved with a community enterprise which has much broader aims and has managed to secure funding from the private sector, public sector grants and from the European Regional Development Fund. Serving two housing estates of around 20,000 people, its aims are 'to raise the economic activity and well-being of the residents.' Long-term unemployment has had a strong impact on the area, which has also experienced housing, environmental and crime-related problems. The project's activities include giving advice to people wanting to set up their own businesses; workshops for local self-employed people; a job centre; childcare provision; and plans for a social club are now ready to be implemented.

Although a community business itself, its aim is to become a holding company with a separate community business division for profit-generating activities. Bill begins his story by describing how far they have progressed:

The Community Business Division is in the process of being set up. The childcare facility is being built right now and has been set up as a wholly-owned subsidiary. My next step on that line was going to be to set up a social club as a wholly-owned subsidiary, but for reasons beyond my control, namely political ones, I can't do that just now. It's all to do with land ownership and allocation and things like that. I actually had the money for it as well, believe it or not; £100,000 offered to me by a brewery. I think at the end of the day I will get my way. The aim of that project is to make money and so make me non-grant dependent. Not non-grant aided, but non-grant dependent. There is a difference.

I started off with a financial background. I spent 20 years working in Africa and then I came back to this country and ran my own small business for a while doing a lot of export to Africa. The recession hit and I found it very difficult to keep operating so I gave it up and saw this job advertised for project manager on a very, very low salary and applied for it.

I came in at that stage effectively as a number two. In the space of about four months the Chief Executive retired. I applied for the job and got it but I changed my title from Chief Executive to General Manager. If you're working on a housing estate area and you're called Chief Executive they expect you to drive a big fat car, sit on your arse and do nothing. As a General Manager they expect you're going to work, and I can assure you that in a job like mine you have to work. I changed the title to make it more acceptable locally; occasionally if I'm dealing with the private sector I do title myself Chief Executive, which is what I am. It depends who I'm talking to.

I work full-time here. I'm only required to work 37 hours a week but probably work somewhere in the region of 50 or 60. Now I'm much better organized. When I first started I worked a lot more. There are so many things happening and so few resources you've got to do a lot yourself. Now there's a full-time admin person; the receptionist is full-time, there are two sharing a job in the Job Centre, and a part-time secretary, plus a seconded officer and then two cleaners. The job shares get employment for more people. All staff, with the exception of myself, are residents and we try, within the Equal Opportunities policy, to recruit only from the estate. We'd only go beyond that if we needed particular expertise which wasn't available locally.

I've got an awful lot of personal satisfaction from working here. You can see you are making a real impact which normally you can't in a job. Here you're not a small cog in some massive wheel somewhere in some fancy big organization, where everything is very easy for you but you don't actually see the end product or see what impact you are making.

For example, when I took over I suppose at most we had about 25 people coming through the door. The only service we really offered was business advice and counselling. Now, we've placed 800 people into work, and some of those people come back in again. They don't always stay in work all the time, and I think it's the personal satisfaction you get when people talk to you and when they come back to you. They appreciate what you're trying to do . . . even if you don't succeed. You can't succeed all the time, but at least they can see you're making an effort and they appreciate that.

You'd be surprised who you get to meet right across the spectrum who are committed to the idea of community action. The networking aspect is really quite important to the survival of the business and I enjoy all that.

I suppose working in a community business is like a cross between working in what would normally be seen as the voluntary sector, but yet you have the benefits of it being a commercial organization.

But I must warn people it can have a serious impact on your social life! It's the hours you have to put in. Fortunately my wife is very committed to this sort of thing as well, so that's very helpful.

The real problem I find is the politics, not with a capital P, but some of the local politics. There are certain people who get involved with these things, not because of what they're going to do for the community but for the ego trip, and that can be quite discouraging on occasions when you're doing your best and people start to get negative and oppose you simply because they haven't been the ones to think of it.

I find it quite disappointing that people cannot put the good of the greater number above individual or sectional interests. I'm talking about people in the local community, be they residents or councillors.

I really enjoy what I'm doing but it wouldn't suit everybody. You've got to be committed to doing this sort of work. Take my predecessor. His background was as a Vice President in one of those big multi-national companies. He was very much a businessman and he was excellent for our company initially in terms of raising private sector interest and contributions, except he couldn't relate to the community. You've got to be able to talk to the prime minister today and a road sweeper tomorrow, and talk to them both the same and gain the respect of both, and that is not necessarily an easy trick to pull; a lot of people can't do that.

So I'd say you've got to be committed to it; committed to what you're doing, and to the community. Ideally you need to have vision. You've got to see what can be done. When I first came up here it was a very low-level job but I could see the potential and, if you like, I had a vision of how it could work, and we're moving towards it and realizing a lot of that vision now. Not all of it – there's more to be done. It's important to realize that it's not going to be just a nine-to-five job; not in any way. I think you also have to be a very open person, almost transparent, so that the community can see you're not trying to con them. You've got to be someone people can believe in.

You also need good people-skills as well, both for your client base, which is your community, and also with the staff who should be equally committed to what you're doing. If you're going to go into something like this you've got to be prepared to take the vision on board, if you like, and go with it.

Bill's community business is doing a significant job of helping to tackle the problems of social deprivation on the two housing estates which it serves. As with Rob, resources are always a

109

problem, particularly the financial resources, but community businesses are commercial organizations and Bill stresses that they do look at returns on investments and value for money.

Many people, if they have heard the term 'community businesses' wrongly associate them with either the voluntary sector or community development. However, in Bill's opinion he sees what they do as making a direct impact on poverty in his area, compared with community development which he thinks tends to make poverty either acceptable or comfortable, without solving it. 'The only way to solve poverty,' he says, 'is to get people jobs or get some sort of economic activity going.'

The community businesses in which both Rob and Bill are involved are doing exactly that. But before you shout 'Eureka' at having found the answer to you and your community's problems, let us have a brief look at some of the pros and cons.

The Pros

Community businesses do have many things going for them and can offer a lot of benefits to both individuals and communities:

- They can provide a way in which to transform an individual's or community's anger or other negative emotion into positive action.
- They enable people to reclaim a sense of power and pride.
- They are a direct method of creating jobs – real jobs.
- They can bring communities together.
- They enable a community to provide for itself the services which it needs.
- They help to generate money for the local community.
- Many local, national and European grants and funds are available to help with start-up costs. Local councils are often only too keen to help support local commercial initiatives, where they might be more reluctant to fund non-income-generating schemes. With the financial support of grants and so on, you do not have to have money of your own before being able to

start the business. It therefore opens the door to 'self-employment' to a great many more people.

- They provide a way in which people can develop their skills and confidence.
- They can provide bridges into other employment, as was the case for some of Rob's colleagues.
- They can provide a step into independent self-employment for some individuals.
- There will probably be lots of initial enthusiasm and energy to help fire the project.

The Cons

It is not all plain sailing, of course. This sort of venture is prey to all the problems associated with any commercial enterprise, as Rob knows only too well with the cashflow problems he has experienced.

- Some potential customers or clients may be wary of trading with a community business because of the misconception that they are less professional than other commercial operations.
- Enthusiasm for the business may start to wane and people may want to drop out.
- You may have to cope with having to discipline people who are your neighbours or friends; or cope with the politics of the situation.
- Fund-raising activities in the early days can be time-consuming.
- There may not be the full complement of skills needed to manage the business successfully.
- Like any form of self-employment, it can be bloody hard work!

Making It Work

If the business is to succeed it needs to be based on a sound commercial base:

- *Establish among you clear aims of what you want to achieve.*
- *Start the action quickly and get everyone doing something, otherwise people soon lose heart.*
- *Find out what funds are available in your area.* Your local council should have that information and be able to point you in the right direction. Think also about approaching the private sector, charitable trusts or potential sponsor. You may be able to generate some money through organizing special fund-raising activities.
- *You may need to beef up on how to run a business if no one has the experience.* You might want to think about approaching local businesses for advice or to suggest an employee with specific skills which you need (like someone in their Marketing Department) to work with you for an agreed period of time.
- *Like any business you must draw up a business plan to show that your enterprise is a viable and serious proposition.* It will help with your fund-raising and sponsorship appeals. It will also help to clarify things and can be used to monitor your progress.
- *As part of the business plan, you must do your market research.* It is vital to establish beforehand whether there really is a demand for your service or product – or whether you just think there is. Subjective assessments are not reliable. You really do need to ask people (your proposed customers) about whether they want what you are planning.
- *Start to develop a high profile in the community – and have plans drawn up to keep it high.*
- *Communication is vital to keep everyone feeling involved in what is going on.* Think about how you could best achieve this.

Many communities have been devastated by the action of major employers as they rationalize, downsize and generally make more people unemployed, which in turn makes the areas in which they are based less economically active. If you are used to working for other people, unemployment can come as a terrible shock. And if you are used to expecting local authorities to be concerned about the social well-being of its communities, it can also come as a shock to realize they have other priorities. By discovering the alternative solution and taking the challenge on board, community businesses offer one way in which to make positive steps forward towards regenerating areas which might otherwise slide further into decline.

Not having come from an entrepreneurial background I used to have the naive belief that somehow the way into enterprise was only open to people who already had money and could invest away like mad in new ventures. That may have been the case, once upon a time; but now, finance is more readily available from many different sources, some public and some private, in order to help other sorts of investors: those who wish to invest in themselves and their communities. A community business might be what you have been looking for to make those investments possible and to find a way in which to work towards securing a better future for yourself – and your local community.

CHAPTER NINE

Working Abroad

As the employment scene changes and evolves, we can start to see new opportunities arise. Our awareness is raised, and where previous generations would have had no need to look further than their immediate locality for employment, present ones are more able and willing to look further afield. Workers move from one side of the country to the other, to where work is available.

Many factors have come together to create opportunities further afield than most of our ancestors would ever have dreamed. People are now realizing that they can push back another barrier to employment – they can seek work in other countries.

Developments

A survey by UK accountants Ernst and Young in 1994 of over 400 organizations across Europe showed they were predicting a significant increase in the world-wide mobility of working people. The globalization of business has obviously played its part in raising the expectation that such movement will take place. As multi-nationals continue to expand operations, and businesses seek out new markets in the rest of the world, offices, branches and factories are opened in countries far and wide – and they all need staff.

Technology has played its part in facilitating the movement of labour, too. For example, the EU has developed a Europe-wide database which enables people to find out about vacancies in countries other than their own. Also, as technology creeps relentlessly into the workplace, new skill-shortages develop. Equally, as workforces move into emerging job opportunities and away from others, skill shortages appear. Despite the high levels of unemployment across Europe, employers are still reporting vacancies which are hard to fill because they cannot find people in their own locality with the appropriate skills. It is because of such difficulties that the EU is backing measures to increase the movement of labour. If Italy does not have the skills it needs, perhaps Spain does; and if Italy can provide the skills France needs, then so be it. Governments seem to be realizing that true flexibility relates to finding ways in which to enable employers to find the people they need, and for employees to access the work they want.

But it is not just in Europe where skill shortages occur. As the developing world moves forward, it too needs expertise and often looks to import skills from other countries, on either a commercial or voluntary basis.

A change in the workforce itself has also played a part in creating this new breed of 'global' workers. Some countries are experiencing an increase in the number of divorced, separated or single people. Without family responsibilities to tie them down, a growing number are using the opportunity to combine work with travel and the chance to experience other cultures.

More people taking early retirement, being made redundant, and being able to take career breaks are also adding to the growing numbers interested in looking at work options in other countries. Experience of other countries while on holiday is bound to help people more easily consider the possibility of working elsewhere. In the UK, approximately 250,000 people leave to work abroad each year, most for temporary periods on contract work which, as we have already seen, is another growth area.

The Opportunities and How to Find Them

There are three broad categories of employment in other countries:

Casual Work

This is work which you might do if you wanted to find a way in which to fund yourself while you travel, or to enable you to toe-dip and find out about what it is like to live and work abroad. Alternatively, you may simply want to live in another country for six months or a year to experience another culture, knowing you will return to your own at the end of it.

Examples: working at summer camps in America, on kibbutz in Israel, on sponsorship programmes for younger adults.

Alternatively, you may have a 'portable' skill or trade (such as hairdressing, catering, book-keeping, or teaching English as a Foreign Language) which enables you to pick up work relatively easily. Work of this sort is normally found in situ by scouring local papers or applying in person to employers. It might also be the most difficult to do legally, since many countries require you to have a work permit. Only if the employer can show there is a shortage of that particular skill in the local labour force can you obtain a permit.

Contract Work

Many jobs in other countries are offered on a contract basis, typically of two years' duration. Skilled, professional and technical posts fit into this category. You may be a sheet metal worker needed in a German factory, or an accountant required in Africa.

Also, work for voluntary organizations in developing countries is on a contract basis, with living allowances set at local pay rates. In the main only skilled and professional people with good experience are recruited to remedy the skills shortages experienced by

116

an area and to help implement specific projects. Some agencies no longer accept recruits with children, but if you fit the bill and are looking for a challenging experience, then voluntary service overseas might be for you. Certainly the reports from people in the UK confirm that it has stood them in good stead, helping them to secure employment once they return from their placement. (*Also see Chapter 10.*)

If you are already in a job, your present employer may have placements available to send you on, but otherwise consider the following ways in which to find such work:

- using databases in public employment offices
- contacting government-sponsored agencies engaged in overseas activities, such as the British Council in the UK
- trade journals
- foreign newspapers
- national newspapers – where employers with overseas operations may advertise
- specialist employment agencies
- professional associations
- writing 'on spec' to employers with offices and operations in other countries
- writing to foreign companies which have links with your own
- contacting foreign embassies, which may be able to help and will certainly have their national newspapers available
- contacting the voluntary organizations operating in your country which export skills abroad.

Permanent Posts

Some advertised vacancies are for permanent positions. Ways of finding such posts are much the same as for contract work, but require a lot more thought before you decide to go since they involve a higher level of commitment from both you and your family. A two-year contract may be manageable if it turns out to be less of a rewarding experience than you had hoped, but it would be very different if you had intended to put down more permanent roots.

The Foreign Experience

John is British and married with two young children. He is an analyst programmer and now works for a large international corporation in France, where he looks after all computing aspects of the company. His post is permanent. I asked him how he came to be working abroad, and what the experience has been like:

We'd always wanted to live and work abroad and I'd been actively looking for about five years. I found this job in a computer magazine. I started it in 1990 and I work full-time, on average nine hours a day.

I think the quality of life we have now is much better than what we had back home. Work-wise there's little difference apart from the cultural problem, which took a while to get over. I get a much better salary than in the UK, although I need it. Yes, a better quality of life and the kids have a better quality of life; the education is a lot better here. And there's more to do at weekends.

We did have some problems on the cultural and language side of things. It took about a year to get used to living in a different culture; the social etiquette one has to pick up in dealing with people. You can offend by having a different cultural attitude. This side of things took a year to come to terms with, but the language side I'm still not comfortable with at work; I can't handle situations as well as I could back home, so I have to enlist the help of a native speaker. I can handle most, but if there's someone there who can speak French better than I can I let them do it. That's one thing, but on the private side you can get upset because you can't do things and sort things out for yourself; you have to get someone to come along. So if you want a loan for a car or something, you lose a certain amount of privacy because the translator has to hear about your finances in order to answer the questions.

The health provision is 100 per cent private here, which has implications with having a family, but although it's free back home I don't think the service is as good. Here, if you need any treatment you get it immediately rather than going on waiting lists.

My wife gets a bit homesick, basically for family and friends, but overall I'm happy working abroad. I think one reason why I might find it easier is that I was brought up abroad as a child, so I think it's in my bones and I think I prefer living abroad. Also, I was always quite distant from my relatives anyway so it hasn't affected me but I think it's affected my wife's side more because they're very close.

For the first year or 18 months the move had an effect on our relationship; not terribly detrimentally but Carol took her frustrations out on me basically; but that's gone now. In the long run it's fine. We knew it was going to be difficult.

Our kids have grown up over here and they are really very French and communicate with each other in French all the time, so it's a great advantage for them to grow up bilingual. That's fantastic.

I've always wanted to work abroad but I could do with a better career path. I could imagine there might be more opportunities available to me in the UK, but that depends on the recession and everything else. I don't know what my next step might be. It depends on what happens in my office here. The company's undergoing a lot of change at the moment. I am concerned about the fact that I've loads of experience but companies would rather take on some young whizz-kid.

For anyone else thinking of working abroad I'd say the first thing to do is to check the job out very thoroughly before you take it because once you're there, you're there, and it's very difficult to get out of it. Even if you can just up sticks and return, it's a very difficult thing to do. We jumped in with both feet, but it's probably best in a family situation for the one taking the job to go for say two or three months on their own so that you can go back if you need to if the job isn't right, although I suspect that if we'd done that then I'd probably be back in the UK now. Basically you've got to get over the first year; some say six months, but I'd say a year, before you can appreciate what it's like.

It helps on the social side if you can go out and meet people, but that depends on the language. We used to go out in the evenings, but we couldn't communicate very easily, then you wind up meeting people who speak your language but whom you wouldn't normally socialize with. You just have to get through the initial period.

For us living abroad was something we'd wanted to do for a long time; it was just a case of when it would happen. If you're thinking about working abroad, you have to think about why. Just be clear about why you're doing it.

On the practical side I'd say that learning the language is certainly worth doing beforehand. Normally a company employing you from overseas should help you out with all the administration problems. If possible, stay for a week or so to see if you like the place you'll be living. We took a long weekend, but I don't think that's long enough. Also, check out the cost of living. We thought my salary was great, until we found out how much it costs to live here.

The move can get complicated if, for example, you have property to leave behind and you have to find someone to manage it, and organize the taxes and so on. There is a lot involved in a move abroad, like making an inventory of the furniture you bring over and getting an ID card, but the company supported us.

Basically I'd say that if you're interested in working abroad then you've just got to do it.

Helen's story is very different, although she echoes many of the points which John raised. An American, she has been working abroad in various countries for almost 30 years on contract postings, whereas John's post is permanent.

She lives with her partner in their present home base in London. I asked her what the motivation was behind her first move to work abroad:

Initially it was just because I'd never been off the North American continent and I was 30 and I thought 'If I don't do it now, when will I do it?' The original intention was to travel for a year; as it turned out I travelled for nine months and then I landed in Wales because a lecturing job was set up for me. So I took a freighter from New York to Tangiers; swanned around Morocco for a bit, then crossed over to Spain and then just pottered around Europe until it was time to go to Wales. It was not a planned career move. A friend of mine had won a scholarship to a college in Wales and when he discovered I was going to take off for Europe he wrote to them and asked if they would take on another American. That was really a pure bit of luck.

So, I settled in this country and then got the opportunity to work abroad in Rome. I just love to travel – I always have, and one way of supporting the travelling has been to find work in various places. I did that in the States when I was younger. I worked on the Eastern seaboard, I worked in the South, I worked in the West . . . I've always worked to support my interest in travel. I can't honestly say I ever planned a career. I like being a journalist and discovered that journalism was one way of supporting my travel addiction. So when the chance came to work in Rome I just jumped at it. It was another part of the world to live in and see what went on there.

The experience of working in different countries has been wonderful. The perspective that you get from living in another culture I think gives you perspective on yourself and a perspective on the culture you came from. I certainly think working in Africa has changed my views, my perspective and, to a certain extent, my values. Nobody has problems until they see Africa. It makes you aware of just how much injustice there is and how incredibly lucky the rich North is. I think experiences like that change your life and I think everybody should do it, not just travel but I think it's important to live there because you can travel very widely without leaving your own country. You simply don't see anything as a tourist. No, that's unfair. You *can* see as a tourist if you have particularly open eyes, but a very large percentage of people travel without seeing.

I think it was Henry Adams who once remarked that tourists see exactly what they brought with them, and I think you have to be somewhere and do your shopping and live there before you can leave the 'baggage' you brought with you behind and actually begin to see what's going on.

I think it's also helped my career. Once you've got a foreign posting on your CV then, if you want to stay in that world, the next lot of employers look more favourably on someone who has worked abroad, and who has presumably survived it and isn't going to be phased by different cultures.

It particularly helps if you've been picking up languages as you go along. Anyone who wants to work abroad now has got to knuckle down and learn some languages because the competition for jobs is such that if you don't have a working knowledge of the country you want to go to then you'll find it very difficult.

Working abroad can also be very good financially. I know people who bank their entire salaries and live on their overseas living allowances. If you've gone overseas with a company they're generally pretty good. On the other hand, if you go on your own you can find yourself living very frugally and very simply, out of necessity.

I should mention some of the disadvantages of working abroad, but it's hard for me to say. I'm not the person to talk to about them because I just love moving about; new places, fresh starts. A friend of mine who is also a wandering sort once said, 'You know it's like being constantly entertained if you're open to it and you absorb it all.'

I can imagine, and I've certainly observed it, that people with families can find it very difficult. If the whole family isn't dedicated to living abroad it can create very severe tensions. I've seen it both ways: husband posted and wife not terribly keen – or the other way around; sometimes with dire consequences when women got posted and have had to confront their husbands with the choice of staying at home and pursuing their careers or going with them. I certainly know of some splits because one or the other partner couldn't cope. It's generally very difficult to post a couple and find suitable work for both.

There's an organization in the UK which runs courses for people about to go overseas, mainly for the partner who won't have a job or something to plug into. It surprised me. I could understand people suffering culture shock in Africa but it surprised me to find people suffering culture shock in Brussels – it's only half an hour away.

I've never experienced culture shock myself. I'm not sure why. I find it quite easy to settle into places. I don't know whether it's because I've never been terribly rooted anywhere, therefore there was nothing to wrench away. I don't know. It's just never been a problem.

But with working abroad you certainly fall out of touch with people at your base, so it's probably more difficult to have deep friendships. I have a lot of friends but they regard me as someone who drops in and out and not someone who's there all the time, so I may not have as many close friends as if I'd lived in the same place for 20 years. I still have contact with the States and go back about once a year.

I think working in other countries certainly makes you more aware. I probably think differently about life in general because I've seen quite a lot. I think it's certainly a humbling experience in some ways – I'd say that about Africa. There's no way that I could cope with adversity the way I've seen Africans cope. It just fills you with awe. I came away from Kenya with that feeling. How do they do it? I just have a feeling that if more people saw it then there'd be an instant redistribution of the world's goods and possibly a whole different attitude from the North. If you go to Africa – and Asia too, to a large extent – you still see what I call family values. People do consciously put other things ahead of material gains and benefits. I remember a guy in the Philippines talking to us about that and saying that when all is said and done all we have is our families; we don't have much but we have our families. They're a lot richer than some of us. I was really interested that that was a conscious value on his part. I think I've seen better ways of living than we've got.

On the relationship front I've been very lucky in that my partner of many years has wanted to come with me, but when we came back from Hong Kong, for the first time he couldn't find a job because the situation here had changed while we were away. Up until then he had been falling in and out of work without too much difficulty. When I went to Brussels he didn't come with me because it is so close and flights are really cheap, so we just flew back and forth at weekends and that worked. But when I went to Nairobi he thought that was a bit far for weekends so he came with me and he was glad he did. But then when we went to Hong Kong things had changed by the time we got back and that was culture shock. That has been a real problem. I think it frightens men particularly to follow their women overseas.

I'd like to go abroad again but I think the only avenue open to me now at 59 is with voluntary organizations. I may be in the wrong trade for that. There is some call for journalism, but not much. A friend of mine has just spent six months in China teaching Chinese journalists, so there are some opportunities, but not a lot. And although opportunities do arise from time to time I would not feel comfortable applying for a job which could be better done by a journalist from that country. I know from time to time there are jobs going in East Africa, which has quite a thriving English press, but then having seen the calibre of journalists in Nairobi I think they should have the jobs.

I'm not looking for jobs at the moment. I think it's my partner's turn to get settled. I think I owe him that.

Because of Helen's many years experience of working abroad in a number of different countries, I asked her what advice she could give to others who might be considering this option:

Don't do it the way I did – just falling in and out of things, particularly if you have a family. I think there has to be an agreement about travelling. If possible, visit the country you're going to be posted to or work in, so you know what you're getting into. I can't stress languages enough. If you can't speak the language of the country you're going to, then you're almost inevitably fated to live in the expat community. I think the benefits of living abroad are in direct relation to the depth to which you can penetrate the culture.

Also, look into finances very carefully. There are some places where you can get done for double taxation. Find out what the cost of living is. I know people who've been caught thinking, wow, all this money, and then they get there and discover that the kind of housing to which they're accustomed is wildly expensive, for example Hong Kong. There's no way I could ever have afforded to live in Hong Kong if I hadn't been on a company salary.

Look at all aspects of it. If you're taking children, find out what the school system's like and find out whether or not the kind of education that is available is going to fit them for taking whatever entrance exams they're going to need for secondary school or university back home. You have to think more long term with children, because even a couple of years in their educational lives can make a huge difference.

I think the people who have been most successful at working abroad have always kept an eye on the base back home. No one knows how long anything is going to last. It's particularly useful if you have a house or a flat. You need something as a base. Just about everyone I know at the news agency had a house or a flat back home. If you're a foreign correspondent you can get kicked out of the country you're in. You've got to have some place to go. Multi-national companies chop and change their operations as well. It's probably essential to keep your eye on the job market back home, too.

If you're sure that working abroad is your real interest there's no harm in acquiring the qualifications that will allow you to do it. Look for portable careers: I thought about English as a Second Language. I would have thought almost anything to do with medicine is portable. Accountancy may be portable, hairdressing, law. With some professions you probably run into accreditation difficulties. Some will rely heavily on languages.

One should also keep one's eye on the political and professional pulse in the country you're interested. Anyone who's considering going to work in the former Soviet Union needs to look very carefully at their extremely shaky economy, for example.

Health is important, and if you have a family then really check out the medical facilities where you're going. If you've any particular problems, make sure you can get a prescription to take along with you for any medication you might need. I don't know if you have to have a stout constitution or not, but you do need to know about the health risks. For example, there is cerebral malaria in Kenya, which is generally fatal; you have to learn what precautions to take. Pay attention to vaccinations and know something about the drugs that you're taking. For example, some of the malaria drugs taken for a long time can have severe side-effects. I'd bone up on health more than I would on anything else. Even in Europe, find out about health insurance in different countries from your own. And never travel or work in the States without millions of pounds' worth of health insurance. If you break a leg there you've financially had it.

Like John, Helen concluded by saying, 'Other than that, I'd say just do it.'

So, two very different experiences from two very different people who have had their own special reasons for choosing to work abroad; for both of them, despite any difficulties they may have experienced, they have been very happy with the choices they have made, and between them they have provided some invaluable insights and advice.

Below is a summary of the pros and cons to consider very

carefully if you intend to pursue this new work option and make working abroad your future career.

The Pros

- Working abroad can give you useful experience, both professional and personal.
- You can learn a lot about yourself.
- If you have children, it can be a wonderful experience for them.
- Being open to considering work abroad increases your job opportunities.
- With casual work, the novelty of a new environment may make the work more acceptable than would otherwise be the case.
- There are expat communities in many major cities, which may help you with adjusting to your new situation.
- Depending on your job, there may be financial benefits.

The Cons

- It might be difficult for family members to adjust.
- Language barriers may cause difficulties unless you learn at least the basics beforehand.
- Voluntary work may take you to areas of risk, both politically and health-wise.
- It can be disruptive for children and their schooling, especially if contracts take you to different locations.
- Long stays abroad may have an effect on your relationships back home.
- There is always the risk of deportation.

Making It Work

Obviously the demands and experiences will vary enormously according to which country you travel to and which country and culture you are leaving, but there are a few points to bear in mind and things to look out for:

- *Think carefully about whether you have the necessary qualities to be able to settle comfortably into another culture.* If you have a family or a partner, talk through very carefully the implications for each of you, including the long-term considerations (such as education) and the more day-to-day and shorter-term considerations.
- *Unless you are planning to emigrate, consider the implications of a more itinerant lifestyle than you and your family may have now.*
- *Do your homework on the country you have in mind, including things like the cost of living.* Keep your eye on current developments taking place politically, economically, etc.
- *Employers are now looking for qualifications, so make sure yours are up to scratch to improve your chance with job applications.*
- *Check out what impact it will have on your tax and insurance position back home.*
- *Check out the health situation and any precautions (including health insurance) you will have to take.*
- *Once you are offered a job, go over the contracts carefully beforehand and establish who will be liable for what expenses, and what sort of assistance your employer will provide.*
- *If you have no languages, consider the implications for you and your family.* How will you cope with socializing and handling your personal business?
- *If you are thinking about taking a career break, what will your position be on your return?* Some organizations will agree to re-employ you, but only at a lower grade.
- *Work out a fall-back position in case things do not turn out exactly as you had planned.* Make sure you have a financial cushion to deal with such an eventuality. You might want to

take Helen's advice and think about maintaining a home base. Property owners can always rent out.
- *Make as long a trip as possible before taking the final plunge to make sure you (and your partner/family) like what you will be going to.*
- *Expect it to take at least six months for you to settle in.*
- *Be realistic.* Working abroad is not the same as holidaying.

Global changes in the business world are opening up more opportunities, not just for the business world itself but also for suitably qualified individuals. It may not appeal to everyone, since some people prefer the security of their own culture. However, for those who are adaptable and are looking to push back those employment horizons, working abroad for at least part of their working lives is worth considering – and certainly, if we are to believe Helen, we could all benefit enormously from the experience.

CHAPTER TEN

Working in the Voluntary Sector

So far we have been looking at opportunities which have been emerging as the result of changes taking place in the world of business, as employers strive to remain competitive in the world's marketplace. However, one area of growth which offers employment possibilities outside the world of commerce and industry is in the voluntary sector.

A Developing Field

Over the years the voluntary sector and the way it operates have changed dramatically in some countries, such as the UK where it was once seen as the preserve of genteel ladies wishing to extend their largesse (and give themselves some meaningful activity). Voluntary organizations now mean big business in some countries, and are a growing industry in others. Many of the larger operations have turnovers in the millions of pounds, dollars or Dm. Yes, there are still the small, local initiatives which exist on the strength of tea parties and jumble sales, but the profile of the voluntary sector is changing and moving towards a much more professional image and approach. Across Europe there are now one in four people involved in volunteering, with slightly more men than women taking part.

Governments have been quick to take advantage of the situation. Looking for as many ways as they can to reduce the consistently high unemployment figures of recent years, they recognize the potential for meaningful employment for many people in this sector of the economy. For example, in the UK an extra allowance is paid to the benefits people receive while unemployed if they take up placements in a voluntary organization.

Some financially hard-pressed governments are also exploiting the growth in this sector in other ways, through cutting back on funding, thus placing the onus on voluntary organizations to find monies from the private sector. Reducing government-funded social provision creates a gap which new and existing organizations are left to fill.

Recognizing the positive role which voluntary organizations can play, in partnership with statutory provision, moves are afoot to encourage the forging of such partnerships within the EU.

Some businesses are also using the demand for expertise in this growing sector to help them cope with managing the effect on its employees of reduced workloads. Instead of cutting their workforces, some commercial enterprises are developing secondment programmes to enable employees to spend time working with voluntary organizations.

Another factor in the growth of this sector in some countries is the change in the social organization and profiles of populations, which is creating a greater demand for social provision. For example, increases in the older population, mobility of the workforce leading to a breakdown of closely linked extended family units, the increasing numbers of people with HIV and AIDS, and so on – all of these demand more and more from the voluntary sector.

With a growing number of voluntary organizations led by increasing demands for their services, the battle to win essential funds is also growing. To be successful they are now having to become more professional in the way they operate, which in turn is creating more job opportunities – both paid and unpaid.

The Opportunities

The changing face of the voluntary sector means that new opportunities are becoming available which may not have been there in the past. Our perceptions of what may be involved in working for a voluntary organization nowadays might be based on out-dated ideas of what goes on in this sector.

Paid Work

The range of skills needed by organizations depends on their size and, to some extent, in which country they are located. For example, the sector is only starting to become more formalized in Greece, while in the Netherlands the voluntary sector is much more highly developed, as it is in Germany. Organizations with a higher profile have a greater need for professional input, although smaller outfits are also realizing that in order to compete effectively for funds and make use of the ones they have, they too must operate in a professional manner – which means finding those skills in professionals and paying them for the work they do.

Here are some examples of opportunities for paid work:

- clerical, secretarial and administrative support
- fund-raising
- co-ordinator posts
- development workers
- counselling
- campaign organizers
- publicity and PR personnel.

Unpaid Work

The benefits of working as a volunteer for an organization are not to be overlooked. It can often provide a useful stepping stone into employment, either within the organization itself, through hearing on the grapevine about other opportunities, or by keeping your CV 'live' and making yourself a more marketable commodity in the competition for jobs.

Unpaid opportunities are almost limitless, since organizations are often grateful for any assistance offered. Depending on where you live, here are some possible openings:

- joining a management committee
- environmental work, including work with animals and archaeology
- hospital work, including running in-house radio stations and helping with beauty care for patients
- international opportunities with some of the larger organizations
- local community work, including helping to organize events
- work with national groups, including campaign work, help with fund-raising, or staffing help-lines
- business advice and expertise is welcomed by most organizations.

Finding the Work

Paid work for the smaller operations is often advertised in local papers, while the larger voluntary organizations place ads in the national press. In addition, you could try writing 'on spec' to the ones you are interested in working for.

The following is a list of places to contact for both paid and unpaid work:

- local volunteer bureau
- residential centres – for example, for elderly people, or those with special needs
- educational centres
- day care or social centres
- religious organizations
- local social services.

In addition, for unpaid work your local library should be able to provide details of local, national and international organizations, and a visit to local hospitals and community centres may indicate what help is needed. Requests for volunteers often appear on community noticeboards.

The Voluntary Sector Experience

We may have preconceived ideas about what it is like to work in the voluntary sector, either as an employee or a volunteer. I spoke to people involved in both capacities to find out what it is really like.

The first person I spoke to was Liz, who manages an employment agency for people with disabilities. It is a part-time post although the demands of the job frequently take her hours almost into the realms of a full-time worker. Liz is half-way through a two-year contract. The voluntary organization she works for is a small, local one, and there are just two of them handling the workload.

Liz began by explaining why she had decided to work in the voluntary sector:

> I suppose I had been thinking about what I could contribute. I knew I had knowledge, skills and experience, but I thought 'Where can I make use of them most?' and I thought of the voluntary sector. Then this job came up and it fitted, in that I needed a job (for money), and I wanted to work, and the fact that it was in a voluntary organization was a bit of a bonus I felt. Prior to this I had worked in the public sector for a number of years.
>
> I found the job partly through the grapevine because I was working part-time for a specialist organization (not a voluntary one) dealing with the same category of people and there is a sort of contact, directly and sometimes indirectly, between all the organizations working in the same or similar field; plus I saw it advertised.
>
> I enjoy working with this client group very much, particularly the ones I've got used to on this particular project, but

generally I think I was getting as much enjoyment working in the non-voluntary sector as in the voluntary.

I must admit I have felt the pressure here of not knowing where the next salary cheque is coming from, and also whether the project can keep going without money coming in. It's the insecurity of not knowing, yet wanting to put ideas into practice; of having vision and ideas of where you want the project to go and being thwarted and restrained because of this constant threat of not knowing whether there'll be any funding. I know this is a very real problem generally now; money is an issue and it has to bring with it restraint, even in business; you know, don't waste resources, use them carefully. I'm aware of all that; we all have to do that in everyday life, but in the voluntary sector it is a hundred-fold more vital than, for example, in the commercial world. It's direct restraint.

Also, I realize that I prefer to belong to a network. I feel less insecure, less out on a limb, and generally safer knowing there are others in the same organization as I am. It's partly to do with support, partly guidance and knowing that there are others doing the same thing; getting feedback from them. In that situation you can also get a measure of how your project is developing and progressing and whether you're doing it right.

I have also worked as a volunteer – I'm still doing it actually, in a different sphere; in a different category. I've been associated with a talking newspaper for four years; that's reading for the visually handicapped.

It's different doing that sort of work in as much that funding and the responsibility for it are not my problem. I am able to do the job, know it is bringing a lot of satisfaction to thousands of people, and I don't have to be concerned with other aspects; I am only doing a job. I'm on a rota with other volunteers and read when it's my turn. I go, I do what I have to do, and I leave knowing and feeling fairly satisfied that I've achieved something without any worries about where the money's coming from. I have worked with visually handicapped people in the past and I realize how important it is for them to have an input from another source, i.e. audio. I think it's an excellent thing and very useful and therefore very satisfying.

For me I would think twice about working in the voluntary sector, really, from the point of view of being a paid employee. There are too many restraints for me, but this may be due to the fact that I've a very commercial background. The transition has been quite difficult for me.

I also didn't expect to have to put in the number of extra hours that I work, but I am such a novice still. I don't think I've had time to step away from it and reach a reconciliation period. I'm still quite close to it and trying to adjust to working in the situation.

I think the only bit of advice I could give to others from my present standpoint is to check on and be aware of the structure of the organization you will be working for, and where you will fit into it; and whether everything is down to you in the job you are considering taking. Really do ask questions about the funding. Ensure that you find out exactly where the main source of funding is coming from, how long it is for; be sure you have a contract and try if possible to find out, and be definitely sure about, who is responsible for the fund-raising.

Find out how much involvement the main committee has and what their contribution is. It's very important, that. Also check whether they know their subject. Some people sit on committees for dubious reasons and if they don't know the field they're supposed to be representing and you're looking for guidance then they really have to know what they're talking about.

Although Liz loves working with her client group, the situation she is in has taught her a lot about some of the difficulties you can encounter, not least of which is what might be called the 'culture shock' she has experienced at finding herself up against many constraints with which she has not been used to dealing. The organization itself is small with few resources, and the gap between herself as a paid worker and the management committee, who are all volunteers with little commercial management experience, is sometimes wide and has proved difficult for Liz to cope with. She is used to a more management-led work environment.

Perhaps sometimes the gains made from working with a particular client-group in the voluntary sector have to be balanced against the difficulties encountered in working for an organization with little management experience – the same situation one might find in any work environment, voluntary or otherwise.

Next I spoke to Pearl, who is retired and lives on her own. I began by asking her how she had found her way into volunteering:

Well, I was bored to tears. I had nothing to do. I was sitting in my room all day, polishing every day. I'd heard someone say they'd been to the volunteer bureau and they said, 'Why don't you go down?' So I went down and that's what started it all off.

Originally I started by working in the snack bar in the community centre of a local church. That went on for three years, then because of problems they decided to close it. I worked two days a week there. If they were short I'd put a few more hours in. Then there's a project for elderly people, and another for people with HIV and AIDS – I go in to them both twice a week, but I find that as one thing drops off something else takes its place. There are odd things that crop up like Christmas parties and so on. Then I went along on a trip with a group of elderly people and cooked for them – and had a fantastic week myself! If things crop up and I'm able to do it, I do it. I suppose I work about 12 hours a week regularly, but if anything else crops up in the mean time then I do it.

As a result of doing voluntary work I've made a lot of really good friends – they even helped me move into my new place. Without them it would have been impossible for me.

Somebody came up with a pair of curtains, and then some-body else with some sheets. All the friends I've made through the volunteer bureau have been great. One chap even turned up with a van to help me move so it didn't cost me a penny. I know now that if I'm ever in a fix or in trouble I know there are people I can talk it out with, to get it sorted.

Whatever you do, you get it back a million-fold when you're volunteering. You get a thousand-fold back in personal satisfaction. But you don't go into voluntary work for what you can get out of it – well, you shouldn't; but you do find that you get paid back a lot more than you'd get paid in your pocket, although you don't get paid back necessarily in money terms. If someone had given me 50 pounds they couldn't have pleased me any better than the man who gave me a bunch of flowers at one of the projects I work for. It was something just so totally unexpected. It can give you more pleasure than having a diamond bought for you because you know that they've no money to throw away and to think they've spent some of it on you . . . well! And there's the advantage of knowing that when you get so as you need some help yourself, you know how to go about asking for it. There could come a time when I need these voluntary services myself.

It's a god-send is voluntary work, both for the people who give it and the people who receive it. I've never been happier.

Doing this sort of work helps you appreciate other people's disadvantages a lot more. When you're just living your ordinary everyday life and don't do voluntary work you don't see people's needs. It makes you appreciate what you've got. Also, I couldn't cope very well with people before, but I can now. It makes you more open, I think.

If you're interested I'd say go in with an open mind; take it as it comes; adjust yourself to circumstances. Working at the church and then at the place for the elderly are two completely different things. You just have to adjust yourself to it. You might go to someone who's a bit proud and a bit stand-offish and you just have to ease your way in – you've got to make yourself fit; don't expect them to fit in with you.

I'd advise anyone that is able to, and has the right attitude towards it, to jump in and do it because they'll find out that they'll reap all the benefits from it. For example, I'd never had anything to do with HIV before, but now it's changed my attitude altogether. It's an education doing voluntary work. Your outlook changes, especially if you get involved with an organization like the volunteer bureau here. I'd do it all over again, and I'll be doing it for as long as I'm able.

I've never had any problems with the work I do, but I know that sometimes they can occur. If they did I'd talk it out with the co-ordinator at the bureau and see what could be done.

But again I'd just say to go and do it. It takes you out of yourself; it makes you meet people; it provides you with interests. And the benefits you get are worth a lot more than money.

I came away from talking with Pearl overwhelmed by her enthusiasm. She could not say enough about what she has gained from volunteering, and I wondered if, had she come to it earlier on in life, whether she wouldn't have made a highly successful paid career out of it. Certainly she has the commitment, and who knows, she may have gone very far indeed.

Here are some more comments from people doing volunteer work:

'I still, in a lot of ways, get more job satisfaction from that work than I do sometimes from my paid work.'

'When I started a family I gave up paid work entirely and worked in the voluntary sector in the inner city, because when you're working for nothing you can continue to make your family your priority because obviously they can't expect things of you if there are things you have to do with the children.'

'I have been an active volunteer for over 20 years, which has also helped me in my (successful) search for paid employment. Voluntary work enabled me to develop my skills and build my confidence and self-esteem. Ultimately, this was a major factor in being able to move on to paid employment.'

Let us summarize some of the pros and cons of working in the voluntary sector, which might help you decide whether or not it is for you.

The Pros

A paid job in the voluntary sector can provide a way in which to combine earning a living with knowing that you are doing something very worth while which contributes to society in a meaningful way. As Liz said, when she found a job in the voluntary sector which was also salaried she saw it as a real bonus.

In addition, there are other advantages to volunteering:

- It is a chance to increase your skills and broaden your work experience.
- It provides a way in which to 'try out' jobs before making a career move. For example, you could work in a shop run by a voluntary group to try out retailing; you could help out in a nursery to see whether you are really suited to working with children.
- It enables you to keep your CV 'live'.
- It gives you a foot in the door and may lead directly, or indirectly, to paid employment.
- It can help you to cope with the difficulties of being unemployed.
- It provides an opportunity to work alongside professionals in the field you are interested in.

And if you talk to someone like Pearl they will convince anyone, without reserve, of the benefits to be gained!

The Cons

Most of the disadvantages seem to relate to paid positions. Because of the element of choice in volunteering, disadvantages are perhaps less likely to be encountered. If a placement does not turn out as you had hoped, you can always find another.

International volunteer work does carry more potential problems than working in your own country. Postings may take you to areas of social or political unrest or where there may be real health risks. Closer to home, the risks appear to be more mundane. Liz pointed us towards some of them:

- Job security can be affected by funding issues.
- You may have to cope with less formal and less well-organized management structures than you are used to.
- The potential for the development of the work you do may be severely curtailed by lack of funds.

Money appears to be a problem whether you work in the private, public or voluntary sector. In commerce it is a question of whether the company is profitable or not and can make enough to keep on staff. In self-employment the same applies (except the staff may be just yourself). In community businesses and co-ops it all hinges on finding seed capital. Voluntary organizations are in a different category entirely. For the majority, the only way in which they can secure their cashflow is to put in a request, or bid, to grant-making bodies – and then keep their fingers crossed. Securing long-term funding is always a problem.

Bearing this in mind, let us have a look at what you might do to help make it work for you, in what is, despite the problems mentioned, a real growth area.

Making It Work

Here are some pointers to bear in mind:

- *Try to have a chat with either the users of the service, or other paid employees.*
- *Consider whether you have the right qualities for the*

paid/unpaid work in which you are interested: motivation, commitment, being good with people, being sensitive to other's needs, good at self-management.

- *If it is unpaid work, check that you are not going to end up out of pocket (unless you are happy and able to).* Ask about expenses.
- *Establish the funding situation before accepting paid posts.* How secure is it, and for how long?
- *Ask about their fund-raising activities – and whether you would be responsible for them or not.*
- *Ensure you receive a very clear job description.* It is easy for workers in the voluntary sector to find themselves being expected to do more than they had initially thought.
- *Find out about what support mechanisms are in place in terms of things like clear line management, secretarial and administrative support.* Is the organization or management committee able to provide the necessary leadership and support?
- *Make sure you understand the managing committee's aims.*
- *You may have to establish clear boundaries with the client group.*
- *If you are to take on a short-term contract, be clear about your own exit strategy.* They may have the money to extend your contract; but then again they may not.
- *Acquiring fund-raising skills through unpaid work will put you in an excellent position to apply for salaried posts, which carry substantial salaries in the larger voluntary organizations.* If you can successfully raise funds you will be like gold dust in this growing sector of the economy.

A Hidden Opportunity

If you can identify a gap in social provision of some sort at either the national or local level, you might want to consider finding ways in which to fill it, either by establishing a local arm to a national operation – or by creating a new voluntary organization altogether. If the thought of handling the project on your own is too daunting, consider whether you could enlist the help of interested others.

If you think this is for you, contact your national agency for voluntary organizations. In the mean time, pay a trip to your local library to see what literature is available, and think about acquiring a useful grounding in the voluntary sector through the unpaid work opportunities available.

CHAPTER ELEVEN

Making It Work

Throughout this book we have looked at the new options arising out of the way in which businesses are reorganizing and introducing new practices to help them cope with escalating pressures to compete. As a result, the times are indeed 'a-changing' for each and every one of us. We cannot fail to feel the impact.

One glance at the jobs advertised in newspapers tells us that the job market is offering options which are very different from those we might have seen, say, 15 or 20 years ago. Then, there may have been the odd variation between jobs, say in the hours worked – 39 for some; 37½ for others, and so on. There was even the odd part-time vacancy advertised. But certainly the majority of ads did not declare that they only wanted you to work for them for six months, a year, or 18 months. In those days it was a little like Ford's statement that you could have any colour car you wanted, so long as it was black. In the job sense, we could work in anyway we liked, so long as it was a nine-to-five job for life. Indeed, many employers would have been horrified if we had suggested that we only intended to stay with them for one or two years. They would have been outraged at such a suggestion, and it would probably have severely jeopardized our chances of securing the job. How times have changed!

Employers are now only too eager to introduce flexible options into their business operations. They want people who are multi-skilled, to give them functional flexibility within their organization so that staff can easily be switched from one task to another.

They also want numerical flexibility so they can manipulate the workforce (and therefore their payroll) to stay in tempo with their production demands. In today's companies there is no room for slack.

The Impact of Change

Change means losing the security of what we have known. This is scary. It is even more scary if the choice has been someone else's and the 'known' has been taken from us (in this case by employers). And it is doubly unnerving when we do not know what is to take its place, or know how to cope with any replacement.

We may be wasting our energies trying to find a secure job for life any more. Sure, some of us might find what may seem to be the regular sort of job we all once knew, but we would be foolish to imagine that redundancy only hits other people.

So where is our security?

Securing Our Future

Fear is often really 'fear of the unknown' – the challenge now is to understand the changes which are taking place in the job markets and then learn how to use those changes to our advantage.

The chapters in this book have endeavoured to look at current changes, the new options being generated as a result, and how you might make them work for you. It may be a difficult transition to make; it calls on us to become more responsible for making our future secure, instead of leaving it to our bosses.

We need to keep an eye on any further changes in the labour market, wherever we live. We need to become pro-active instead of reactive – instead of waiting until the house of cards falls down, we must change our attitude. As much as we need employers if we are to stay in paid employment, employers equally need a work-force, and one which can respond to its requirements.

Once we know the rules of the game, we can more easily enter on a more level playing field. Not only do we need to be willing to make ourselves multi-skilled and adaptable, we also need to realize that there are growth areas in some forms of employment which we may be able to use to further our own advancement.

Our security may lie in creating our own safety net. A one-bag approach puts us at risk, should that one bag burst. If our single income-generating job disappears, so too does our major source of security. To create a more secure position for ourselves we might think of spreading the risk around and designing our working lives so that we have more than just the one income-generating activity. Not only does this approach create a better situation for ourselves and our families, it also means we can respond to the opportunities which are emerging.

The Portfolio Approach

In Chapter 2 we looked at developing a portfolio of part-time jobs to create a more secure work environment for ourselves. This concept can be extended beyond the boundaries of just part-time jobs and used to create a mix-and-match approach embracing many job options.

A portfolio approach to our working lives enables us to adapt as circumstances or our own needs and interests dictate. By nature we are dynamic beings; amassing a collection of work interests is one way of creating an environment which can respond to that dynamism. Just as employers need to have the flexibility to respond to fluctuating demands on productivity, so do we need to have flexibility to be able to respond to our changing natures and situations in life. A job or work environment which suits us at one point in time may not fit the bill further down the line. In the portfolio approach, a single element can be dropped and replaced by something more suited to the new direction in which we wish to go. Space can be made to enable us to share in childcare, or investigate self-employment options, or simply to create more of a breathing space to balance our lives.

Portfolio working gives us more freedom, more control and yes, more responsibility. We now have to learn to plan ahead a bit more, because we have learned that we cannot take our jobs for granted any more. We may have to take on board some responsibility for our own professional development. As workers in the peripheral sector we may find ourselves excluded from access to training by employers. We may need to plan to make spaces in our working year, continually to update our skills. We could plan to use anticipated 'down time' for this, such as a gap between when one short-term contract ends and another begins.

Infinite Possibilities

Well, not quite infinite, but there are many ways in which the new work options can be combined to create a tailor-made situation which suits your specific lifestyle and aims:

- part-time work that is also self-employed work
- part-time work on a short-term contract in the voluntary sector combined with self-employment (the option I once went for)
- self-employment as a teleworker combined with a return to study
- job sharing an overseas post in the voluntary sector for two years
- setting up a community business combined with part-time work, then replacing one of the options with a return to study to enable you to move on into full-time, short-term contract work in the voluntary sector
- a co-operative based on teleworking, operating on a sub-contract basis.

Whatever your needs, whatever flexibility you (and your partner and family) require, is open to investigation. Of course, necessity may dictate some of your choices at various points in your working life. This happens to most of us. There are also risks involved in some of the options mentioned, which need to be studied carefully. Unfortunately there is no perfect solution and no absolute guarantees for us to depend on. What we can do is look at what we want out of life and how we can best move forward to those goals, using the skills, vision and experience we now have available to us.

Charles Handy believes 'necessity will make portfolio workers of us all in the end.' He refers to what he terms the 'Third Age' in life, between the ages of about 50 and 75 (that is, the years in which we may expect to retire). As he points out, many people are taking early retirement, state pension provision is likely to shrink, and the need for additional income may be a very real possibility for many of us. At some stage in our lives we may all come to the point where combining different career elements becomes the norm. The majority of the elements may be income-generating, but some may not – it is up to you. Kate, as you may remember from Chapter 5, combined studying law with a job share, while Sarah used a job share to help her find her way back into the core workforce. Her full-time income as a professional enabled her partner to leave his job, go back into full-time study and then facilitate his own career change.

The changing work situation is here. More changes may be in the pipeline, created through developments in technology, amendments to legislation or changes in world economies. But as the people interviewed have shown, instead of feeling left on the sidelines there are positive ways in which to take advantage of the new opportunities on offer, and to start making them work for *you*.

Resource List –
Useful Addresses and Further Reading

CHAPTER 1
The Empty Raincoat, Charles Handy (Hutchinson, 1993)

CHAPTER 2
Part-time Work, Judith Humphries (Kogan Page, 2nd edn 1986)

Part-time Careers Ltd
10 Golden Square
London W1R 3AF
0171–437 3103
An employment agency specializing in part-time vacancies. Check your local *Yellow Pages* for others.

For information on employment rights and benefits relating to part-time working contact your local Job Centre or Citizens Advice Bureau. Addresses in your local telephone directory.

Australian Association of Career Counsellors
43 Godfrey Road
Artarmon
Sydney NSW
61 2 415 3216

CHAPTER 3
Executive Standby Ltd
Dodd's Lane
27 Preston Street
Faversham

Kent ME13 8PE
01795 530830
An employment agency which specializes in placing people who have senior or boardroom experience in interim management positions. Check your local *Yellow Pages* for other similar agencies.

For information on employment rights and benefits relating to short-term contract work, contact your local Job Centre or Citizens Advice Bureau. Addresses in your local telephone directory.

CHAPTER 4

The Age of Unreason, Charles Handy (Century Hutchinson, 1989)

Home Is Where the Office Is, A. Bibby (Hodder and Stoughton, 1991)

European Journal of Teleworking (quarterly journal; Addico Publishing Ltd); 0966–7458 (ISSN); tel: 01736 332736

The Indispensable Guide to Working from Home (British Telecom). Free guide; tel: 0800 800854

National Association of Teleworking
The Island House
Midsomer Norton
Bath
Avon BA3 2HL
01761 413869

Telecottage Association
WREN Telecottage
Stoneleigh Park
Warwickshire CV8 2RR
01203 696986 or Compuserve 100114,2366

CHAPTER 5

Job Sharing: A practical guide, Pam Walton (Kogan Page, 1990)

New Ways to Work
309 Upper Street
London N1 2TY
0171–226 4026

For information and advice on job sharing as well as other flexible working arrangements. The organization also operates a register of people who are looking for suitable job share partners.

CHAPTER 6

101 Ways to Start your Own Business, Christine Ingham (Kogan Page, 1992)

Working, Studs Terkel (Wildwood House, 1975)

Working Well at Home, Christine Ingham (Thorsons, 1995)

There is a wide range of other books available on various aspects of setting up and running your own business, many of which may be available in your local library.

Home Run, subscription magazine for self-employed people who work at home. Available from:
Home Run
79 Black Lion Lane
London W6 9BG
0181–846 9244

Also check out the growing number of magazines for the entrepreneur which can now be found in most large newsagents.

The network of *Business Links*, one-stop advice shops for the self-employed or those intending to set up a business, is now established. Contact your local Job Centre for details or see your local telephone directory.

Australian Small Business Association
28 Mary Aubn
Sydney NSW
61 2 649 8298

CHAPTER 7

The Workers' Co-operative Handbook, Peter Cockerton and Anna Whyatt (ICOM, 1986)

Industrial Common Ownership Movement (ICOM)
Vassalli House
20 Central Road
Leeds LS1 6DE
0113–246 1737/8
Your first point of contact if you are interested in setting up a co-op.

NSW Registry of Co-operatives
1500 Bankstown
NSW 2200
61 2 793 0525

International Co-operative Alliance
15 Route des Morillons
1218 Grand Saconnex
Geneva
Switzerland
(022) 929 88 88

CHAPTER 8
Community Start Up, Caroline Pinder (National Extension College).
Can be ordered direct from:
National Extension College
18 Brooklands Avenue
Cambs CB2 2HN
01223 316644

Directory of Grant-making Trusts, Charities Aid Foundation. Available
in most libraries.

Community Development Foundation
60 Highbury Grove
London N5 2AG
0171–226 5375
Your first point of contact for advice and information if you are
interested in getting a community-based initiative off the ground.
(See also resources listed above for chapters 6 and 7.)

CHAPTER 9
How to Get a Job Abroad, Roger Jones (How to Books Ltd, 1991)
Work your Way Around the World, Susan Griffith (Vacation Work, 1993)

There are a number of other books available which concentrate on
specific countries or aspects of working abroad. Check them out at your
local library or bookstore.

Overseas Jobs Express (subscription magazine)
Premier House
Shoreham Airport
West Sussex BN43 5FF
01273 440220

British Council
10 Spring Gardens
London SW1A 2BN
0171–930 8466
The British Council exists to promote cultural, educational and
technical co-operation between Britain and other countries. It employs
some 4,000 staff, who mainly work outside the UK.

CHAPTER 10
Volunteer Centre UK
Carriage Row
183 Eversholt Street
London NW1 1BU
0171–388 9888
For information about volunteering and the opportunities available in
your area.

REACH
Bear Wharf
27 Bankside
London SE1 9ET
0171–928 0452
REACH finds part-time, expenses-only jobs for retired businesspeople
or other professional men and women who want to use their skills to
help voluntary organizations with charitable aims. This free service is
available for jobs anywhere in Britain.

Voluntary Service Overseas (VSO)
317 Putney Bridge Road
London SW15 2PN
0181–780 2266
VSO is the UK's main organization for volunteering opportunities
abroad.

Volunteer Placement and Resource Service
12 Wentworth
Manly
Sydney NSW
61 2 977 1066

Australian Volunteers Abroad for Work Overseas
61 2 550 3955

Index

Of further interest . . .

Working Well at Home

Managing the ups and downs
of working where you live

Christine Ingham

Working at home is often the starting-point for many who become self-employed. However, problems can often arise out of working in the place where you live, including isolation, lack of motivation, conflicting demands and relationship problems. Left unresolved, they may affect the ultimate success or failure of the venture. Christine Ingham, herself a home-based worker, combines suggestions on how to manage both the personal and interpersonal difficulties with the recommendations of others who, between them, have over 50 years' experience of working at home.

Whether freelance, consultant, entrepreneur or just thinking about it, *Working Well at Home* is a personal and practical guide which can help. Home-based employees, including the growing number of teleworkers, will also find much of relevance here.

Coping with Change at Work

Susan Jones

It was not so long ago that our place of work provided us with a stable environment when other areas in our lives were in turmoil. This no longer is the case. Changes at work, whether technological, a promotion, a new job, a redundancy, a takeover or a new management style, can be highly stressful.

This practical guide aims to enable people to make sense of their new work situation and to excel. Checklists, step-by-step guidelines and real life case studies are included, making the book invaluable for those going through a period of transition. Other issues covered include self-esteem, status, control, management issues, career progression, risk and reward.

Intended primarily for people who are going through a period of change, whether at management or staff level, this guide is also helpful for anyone who wants to learn more about this topic.

How to Think on Your Feet

Marian K. Woodall

- Have you ever been caught off guard in a meeting?
- Stumped by a question during a sales call?
- Suffered an embarrassing silence during an interview?
- Thought of the perfect response – after the conversation?

You are responsible for one half of every conversation you have . . . in business, in community affairs, at home . . . and you must be able to respond appropriately and confidently in order to succeed. This book will teach you how to think – and speak – on your feet. The author, a top lecturer and seminar leader in business communications for 24 years, shares her experience with you and shows you how to:

- Answer questions impressively – even if you don't know the answer
- Buy time so that you can think before you speak
- Retain composure when facing difficult questions
- Polish your delivery skills

Everybody needs to be able to communicate well. Using proven theory, on-target strategies, and practical examples, Marian K. Woodall will help you improve your end of the conversation.

Coping with Stress at Work

How to stop worrying
and start succeeding

Jacqueline M. Atkinson PhD

If you:

- Work better to a deadline
- Leave things to the last minute, then do them in a panic
- Constantly feel in a rush
- Feel full of dread at the thought of going to work
- Often skip lunch
- Stay late at the office, or take work home
- Get tired, irritable and depressed

then you are suffering from stress. And if your way of dealing with it is to have another cup of coffee or reach for a cigarette, switch on the television or pour yourself a stiff drink you are making the problems worse.

This book offers original and varied ways of combating stress in the workplace. It will help you deal sensibly and practically with stress in a way that suits you and your working environment. You will discover your own stress triggers and look at resolving and easing stressful situations; you will learn how to relax, manage your time, and deal with problems before they deal you an ulcer.

How to Talk so People Listen

Sonya Hamlin

- Have you ever come away from a meeting knowing that you haven't made your point effectively?
- Have you ever made a presentation and felt audience attention slipping away?
- Do you sometimes find it difficult to understand your business associates and meet them halfway?
- Do high–powered encounters with the boss simply put you on the defensive?

If any of these problems sound familiar, then *How to Talk so People Listen* is full of the advice and help you need. You can identify what your listener wants from an encounter, and ensure that everyone gets the best possible results. Find out the best time to hold meetings – to lunch or not to lunch? – or how to gain prior knowledge of audiences and motivate them through self-interest.

This book exposes our preconceptions about communicating in the workplace and brings a new, highly effective dimension to this complex world. Sonya Hamlin is an Emmy-Award-winning chat show host and heads her own communications consultancy – she has acted as an adviser to the chief executive officers of such companies as American Express and Polaroid.

I Want More

Straight talking advice on how to
get what you want

Stephanie Myers

As a black girl growing up with eight brothers and sisters in
Bristol, Stephanie Myers learnt from an early age about
racial abuse, poverty, unemployment, discrimination and
heartache.

With cheerful determination she fought back, and by the
age of 26 had formed her own highly successful training
company. Her 'tell 'em like it is' approach has helped thousands of people, from teenage ex-offenders to directors of
multi-national companies.

In this, her first book, she offers a no-nonsense guide to
getting more of what you want – be it respect, job satisfaction, money confidence or love. No dramatic efforts are
required: the key is in small improvements and gradual
changes.

If any book can help those struggling against oppression,
poverty and unhappiness, then this is it.

How to Think Like a Millionaire

Who better to teach you success than those
who have made millions themselves?

Charles-Albert Poissant

In this amazing book, which may be your first step on the road to millions, Charles-Albert Poissant examines the factors that lead to success. He looks at 10 of the world's richest self-made men, including Henry Ford, Paul Getty and Stephen Spielberg, and demonstrates that their success was no accident – they all shared certain principles and attitudes. Now you have the opportunity to learn their secrets and use them for your own success.

From their experiences you can learn:

- The major prerequisites for becoming rich
- That age, education and lack of capital are irrelevant in attaining wealth
- The art of positive thought and positive action.

Mindstore

The ultimate mental fitness programme

Jack Black

Have you ever looked at people who are successful, either socially or professionally, and thought to yourself, 'How gifted', 'How lucky'?

Yet the truth is, 'How unlikely'. Either intentionally or subconsciously, successful people have developed a programme of mind-management which has enabled them to be different. This power is present in everyone, not just a 'gifted' few.

Jack Black, a leading motivational speaker and the founder of MindStore, has dedicated his life to discovering the techniques, beliefs, strategies and visions of success.

For the first time in book form, his message is now available to all. Entertaining, dynamic and above all easy to learn, discover for yourself how to:

- Master emotions, finances and relationships
- Let go of your 'I can't' philosophy
- Gain renewed energy for life
- Manage stress
- Achieve your dreams.

WORKING WELL AT HOME	0 7225 3035 8	£6.99	☐
COPING WITH CHANGE AT WORK	0 7225 3130 3	£6.99	☐
HOW TO THINK ON YOUR FEET	0 7225 2963 5	£4.99	☐
COPING WITH STRESS AT WORK	0 7225 3095 1	£4.99	☐
HOW TO TALK SO PEOPLE LISTEN	0 7225 2958 9	£6.99	☐
I WANT MORE	0 7225 3186 9	£5.99	☐
HOW TO THINK LIKE A MILLIONAIRE	0 7225 3105 2	£6.99	☐
MINDSTORE	0 7225 2994 5	£5.99	☐

All these books are available from your local bookseller or can be ordered direct from the publishers.

To order direct just tick the titles you want and fill in the form below:

Name: _____

Address: _____

_____ Postcode: _____

Send to: Thorsons Mail Order, Dept 3, HarperCollins*Publishers*, Westerhill Road, Bishopbriggs, Glasgow G64 2QT.
Please enclose a cheque or postal order or your authority to debit your Visa/Access account –

Credit card no: _____

Expiry date: _____

Signature: _____

– to the value of the cover price plus:
UK & BFPO: Add £1.00 for the first book and 25p for each additional book ordered.
Overseas orders including Eire: Please add £2.95 service charge. Books will be sent by surface mail but quotes for airmail despatches will be given on request.

24 HOUR TELEPHONE ORDERING SERVICE FOR ACCESS/VISA CARDHOLDERS – TEL: 0141 772 2281.